How the New Stock Exchange Works

About the Author

Colin Chapman is a leading financial writer and broadcaster. A former economics correspondent of BBC TV News, and a presenter on BBC radio's Financial World Tonight, he is now publisher and editor of the weekly newspaper Financial Adviser, and Managing Director of Financial Television Limited. Earlier, in Australia, he was Deputy Editor of *The Australian*, and correspondent for the *Financial Times* and the *New York Times*. He lives with his wife, Susan, in London.

THE OBSERVER

HOW THE NEW STOCK EXCHANGE WORKS

Colin Chapman

HUTCHINSON BUSINESS BOOKS
LONDON MELBOURNE AUCKLAND JOHANNESBURG

First published in 1986 by Century Hutchinson Ltd,
Brookmount House, 62–65 Chandos Place, Covent Garden,
London WC2N 4NW

Century Hutchinson Australia Pty Ltd
16–22 Church Street, Hawthorn, Melbourne, Victoria 3122

Century Hutchinson New Zealand Ltd
PO Box 40–086, 32–34 View Road, Glenfield, Auckland 10

Century Hutchinson Group South Africa Pty Ltd
PO Box 337, Bergvlei 2012, South Africa

Second edition 1987 (paperback)

British Library Cataloguing in Publication Data

Chapman, Colin, *1937–*
How the new stock exchange works: city life
after the big bang.—2nd ed.
1. Stock exchange *(London)*
I. Title
332.64'24212 HG4577

ISBN 0–09–172552–6

Set in Linotron Sabon by
Input Typesetting Ltd, London SW19 8DR

Printed in Great Britain by
Guernsey Press

Contents

Acknowledgements

The number of people who have helped me is too great to be listed in full. I have benefited from the assistance of hundreds of people in London, New York, Tokyo, Hong Kong and Sydney to put together this second and updated edition of how the new stock markets work. Incidentally it is no longer possible to talk of a Stock Exchange as one physical building, for a very low proportion of trading takes place on the floor, but electronically and by telephone, although most of those buying and selling equities in London do so under the aegis of the Exchange, and operate within its rulebook.

There are a few people who deserve special thanks: Luke Glass of the Stock Exchange, whose patience in dealing with endless questions was invaluable; Michael Hughes of Barclays de Zoete Wedd who was always at the end of the telephone to offer wisdom, and friends at the BBC, the *Financial Times, Asian Business*, and *The Observer*. I have also been given considerable help by that invaluable institution, the City Business Library.

For historical perspective I have drawn partly on material culled from the archives researched by Professor E. Victor Morgan and W. A. Thomas, in their comprehensive *The Stock Exchange: Its History and Functions*, and on the very readable account of the early years in *The Stock Exchange Story* by Alan Jenkins, which I commend to those who would like to know more about the activities in and around Throgmorton Street in the eighteenth and nineteenth centuries. I am grateful to Vickie Smiles and Nora Campbell for researches on my behalf.

Finally I wish to thank my family for their continued encouragement and tolerance, particularly my wife, Susan Grice, and my mother, Marjorie Chapman, who both made many helpful suggestions and read the manuscript with the perspective of many in Britain who are like themselves –

hard-pressed small investors, both hopeful and dubious about the prospects for the new stockmarkets.

1 The Big Bang

'It is like a Franz Kafka novel, trying to plan the future of one of our great national institutions, without knowing what is in store' – Sir Nicholas Goodison, chairman of the Stock Exchange.

'The main impact of the Big Bang theory has been an unprecedented and unholy game of musical chairs. Instead of a Who's Who, the City badly needs a Who's Where?' – Robert Heller, publisher and writer.

The City of London, a damp and unprepossessing square mile of grey stone and cement built on Thames mudflats, has been the world's most important financial influence since the days of the cargo cult. It is a great survivor. London Bridge may have burned down, but the City survived the holocaust of the Great Fire. Warring armies skirmished in what are now known as the Home Counties, but never scaled the City's walls. Hitler's Blitz left the Square Mile badly scarred but trading continued amid the sirens and the firefighting. When invasion seemed imminent, City men packed their wives and children off to the Welsh hills or to country farmsteads, but stayed at their desks, minding the nation's money shop.

The City, almost miraculously, has also survived Britain's post-war economic and political decline. While our heavy industry has crumbled – and much of manufacturing industry has had to fight for survival – the banks and other financial institutions that provide most of Britain's invisible exports have thrived and prospered. Britain is still merchant banker to the free world, and foreign governments, corporations and individual potentates daily entrust gold, silver and dollars to financial houses in the City of London.

Each day about £50 billion worth of foreign currency changes hands in London, yielding the banks and exchange dealers a fortune in commission, and making the City the dominant market in foreign exchange, with one third of world business.

London's financial pull and strength are all the more surprising, given the sustained assault on the City by the politicians. For the best part of three decades, large sections of the Labour movement – and not only the Left – have berated the City with the kind of passion that only comes when hatred is mixed with envy. Labour Governments have threatened the City with reform, perhaps even overthrow, and even those at the centre of the Labour Party have not shied from expressing emotive desires – for instance, Denis Healey's wish to squeeze and squeeze 'until the pips squeak'. Socialist desires to bring the City to heel have resulted in there being an almost continuous state of inquiry into the activities of the Square Mile. But despite the probing of the commissions of inquiry chaired by Lord Radcliffe and Lord Wilson, the City, until 1986, remained intact, and largely responsible for policing its own affairs. Although innumerable scandals have at times appeared to threaten its independence, it has managed until now to avoid coming under the supervision of a powerful Securities and Exchange Commission, such as exists in the United States, in Australia and some other financial markets.

On the surface, then, in the second half of the 1980s, with a friendly Conservative government in power at Westminster and left-wing politics outlawed to decaying urban boroughs, the City is thriving. There is visible evidence of prosperity at every corner. At lunchtime the best restaurants are usually fully booked, despite strenuous attempts to price themselves out of business.

With a ten-year bull market, trade on the Stock Exchange has been booming. Office space is at such a premium that rents in the City are higher than on Wall Street, and this affluence is starting to spread into neighbouring Islington and Dockland.

Yet the City does face a crisis – and one that is very different from crises in the past – for London's position as a financial centre is under threat from within, through what has come to be known as 'Big Bang'. In late 1985, it was hard to find any banker or stockbroker, or indeed any other financial luminary prepared to talk about much else. 'The only thing I know that is going on is that no one knows what the hell is going on', a director of the merchant bank, Baring Brothers and Co. Ltd, said to me over lunch. 'It is chaos.'

The catalytic changes for 'Big Bang' seem, on first examination, harmless enough. Basically all that happened was the abolition of fixed commission for the buying and selling of shares on the London Stock Exchange, and the removal of traditional barriers between the principal operators in any financial deal – banks, merchant banks, stockbrokers, discount houses, and financial and investment services' companies. Not enough, you may think, to rock the collection of established national institutions that make up the City. Yet the changes are the consequences of other forces which have swept through the world financial community, the chief of which have been the new instant electronic communications and a shift of economic power from the Atlantic to the Pacific.

As veteran banker Stanislas Yassukovich, brought in by the giant American securities house, Merrill Lynch, to head their European operation and guide it through the storms of 'Big Bang', put it to me: 'The real upheaval has been caused not by what has gone on in the Stock Exchange, but by the revolution in information technology. When any change or announcement is passed round the world in seconds, the old fashioned business of trading on a floor becomes irrelevant.'

Growth in the European economies has been dwarfed by the rising prosperity of the United States and Japan, where both sunrise and smokestack industries have been able to take advantage of huge spending on research and development, made impossible in Europe by the limited horizons of many nationalistic companies and the many impediments to growth created by several layers of bureaucracy. Companies like IBM, General Motors, General Electric, ITT, Boeing, Toyota, Mitsui, Nissan, Sony, Fanuc and Fujitsu have enjoyed enormous worldwide growth, and their added values have contributed to surplus funds being available for investment on a global scale. In addition, thanks to low inflation and high growth, the pension funds of both the United States and Japan have built up huge surpluses, which have to be invested. These investors will only use financial houses outside their own country if it is worth their while.

The requirements for money centres to provide the raft of financial services needed to support the world's corporate giants and traders are very constraining. The telephones and computer systems have to work, for example, which rules out most third world capitals. Financial centres need to be in countries which have democratically elected, stable governments, and, unhappily, there are not too many of these. You cannot expect to be entrusted with other people's money if there is an above-average chance of a band of crazy colonels or young revolutionaries swaggering through a banker's door toting machine guns. Nor is it any use establishing a financial centre in a place where the inhabitants persistently refuse to accept that English is the internationally preferred language. A financial centre also needs to be able to call upon a pool of educated professionals and operators, and this dictates the need for a place which can offer a better-than-average lifestyle. Finally, a relaxed regulatory atmosphere is crucial.

Only a handful of cities meet these criteria. They are, in alphabetical order, Amsterdam, Brussels, Frankfurt, Hong Kong, London, New York, Sydney, Toronto, and Zurich. Of these New York and Tokyo stand out as representing the two most powerful economies, and their very strength limits the expansion of other markets in the same time zone.

Between them the New York and Tokyo stock markets have a market capitalization three times the size of all the rest of the world's stock markets put together, including London's. Share markets in the United States, of which the largest is the New York Stock Exchange, account for a market value of $US 1,783 billion. Far behind comes Japan with shares valued at a total $731bn., but still larger than all the markets in Europe combined. Of Europe's $700bn. market capitalization, London has the most important market, worth $302bn., with West Germany valued at $118bn., Switzerland worth $63bn., and France, Italy and the Netherlands each around $50bn.

So assuming, in this new global money game, that one centre is needed to bridge the gap between New York and Tokyo, the obvious choice is London. But although turnover in London is more than half the total trading of the 15 other European bourses, its volume does not make it a truly European exchange. Only 65 of the 450 foreign companies quoted in London are continental European, most, more than 200, are American, who could easily switch their listing elsewhere. The City does have potential rivals. With major changes planned in the German financial system, any faltering or major policy switch in London, such as the election of a left-wing Labour Government, could easily lead to the emergence of Amsterdam or Frankfurt as a rival, with Zurich dominating the banking industry.

This discussion assumes, of course, that you need a major financial centre in the middle time zone, and it is an assumption that can no longer be made with any certainty. At present New Yorkers are still asleep when trading stops on the Tokyo Stock Exchange, but the new dealing systems mean that it is no longer necessary for trading to take place as a result of dealers gathering in a hall to shout at each other, like farmers at a cattle auction.

The Eurobond Market

The role of the stock market in raising money for the expansion and development of companies whose shares are listed on their Exchange is also being threatened by international capital-raising, conducted in a deregulated manner across international boundaries. The most interesting example of this is the Eurobond market. Any large and creditable multinational corporation can now borrow money on a global scale by issuing bonds – fixed interest securities denominated in a currency of its choice repayable over a long period.

Buying and selling international bonds was a natural development of international currency trading. For years currencies have been traded against each other by telephone, with active markets in all the financial centres mentioned earlier, and the end of restrictions on the flow of money in and out of currencies led to the explosive growth of what are now known as the Euromarkets. These developed from the trade in American dollars, whose owners had no desire to repatriate them to the United States and provided a pool of money for investment. The Eurodollar market gave birth to the Euroyen market; and now the Euromarkets embrace a host of other currencies, as well as hybrids such as the European Currency Unit, or ECU.

It was only a short time before straightforward currency loans developed into bond finance, as foreign governments, multinational agencies and large corporations found it convenient to borrow from this pool of money. Now the Eurobond market is very large and very sophisticated. Transnational corporations find Eurobonds a tax-efficient way of raising money. They set up subsidiaries in Luxembourg or the Netherlands Antilles to issue them, and back the bonds with the guarantee not only of their own international reputation, but also that of the group of merchant banks or finance houses who act as underwriters. The money raised can be switched to any part of the world where the company needs it.

One advantage, at least for some of those who invest in Eurobonds, is their anonymity. There is no central register, which inquisitive journalists or private detectives may probe, in order to establish a bondholder's wealth. Bonds are obtained from the register of the company or government issuing them, usually via the dealer.

The first that most investors know about a new bond issue is after it has taken place, when an advertisement – known as a 'tombstone' because of its shape and general greyness – appears in *The Financial Times* and *The Wall Street Journal*. *The Financial Times* of 19 December 1985 contained several. One announced that Heron International Finance NV, registered in The Hague, had issued ECU 60m. 9⅜ per cent guaranteed retractable bonds, repayable between 1992 and 1997. The bonds, said the tombstone, would be 'unconditionally guaranteed jointly and severally' by Heron International NV, or Curacao in the Netherlands Antilles, and Heron International plc, of London. Beneath this statement was a list of banks. Three of them, Banque Indosuez, Banque Bruxelles Lambert SA and Lloyds Merchant Bank Ltd were displayed across the top of the list. Beneath were the names of 18 more banks, five of them European, four American, four Japanese, and three British.

What this advertisement told the reader familiar with these

tombstones was that Gerald Ronson's Heron Group had raised a sum of money equivalent to 60m. European Currency Units of Account – about £33m. – by issuing bonds at just under 10 per cent interest. In the months ahead if general interest rates were to go down, the value of the bonds would go up, because of the yield, and vice versa. The three lead banks named had organized the capital raising, and with the other banks listed were guaranteeing to find buyers. In fact, even before the advertisement appeared, bond salesmen at each of the banks would have contacted major institutional investors offering parcels of the bonds for sale.

In the same issue of *The Financial Times*, tombstones reported an ECU 100m. issue for the French nuclear power utility Centrale Nucléaire Européenne à Neutrons Rapides SA at 9 per cent, $500m. for the International Bank for Reconstruction and Development, and $75m. for Japan's Sumitomo Chemical Company.

Belying their name, the Euromarkets are nothing whatever to do with the European Community, and although the European Currency Unit has its attractions as a denominator currency, it is dwarfed in volume by bonds denominated in other currencies, such as the US dollar, the German Mark, or the Japanese yen. Nor is most of the action in Continental Europe; the centre for Euromarket activity is London. There is, however, no trading floor, and almost all the business is carried out by telephone, with the major Eurobond dealers working from large electronic dealing rooms. Nor are the principal operators British, but American and Swiss, with three groups dominant – Merrill Lynch, Goldman Sachs, and Crédit Suisse First Boston. Back in 1970 there were only 163 banks operating in the Eurocurrency market in London, accounting for a turnover of $35bn.; by 1984 the number of foreign banks had grown to 403; turning over $460bn.

Unfortunately for the Stock Exchange most of this activity totally by-passed it, much to its chagrin. An even greater irritation was the introduction of a new instrument – the equity-convertible Eurobond – whereby a company raised loan finance through the issue of a ten-year interest-bearing bond, but gave the bond-holder the option of retrieving his capital through the allocation of equities in the company. Thus shares in both British and international companies were issued in large quantities without any Stock Exchange getting a sniff of the deal.

Commercial Paper

Another development which has by-passed stockmarkets has been the development of a commercial paper market,, both on a global and British scale, brought about because large and prestigious corporations realized that the cost of short-term borrowing through the banking system was far too high. Why pay high interest rates, they asked themselves, when they could borrow directly from investment institutions who would be only too pleased to lend them surplus funds short-term. After all many commercial multinationals could be considered a safer bet than banks, with their record of misjudgement on Third World loans?

Commercial paper in fact is nothing much more than IOU's – backed by the good name of the corporation or country issuing the IOU. They are offered to investors at a discount which reflects current interest rates, and when they mature, which is usually over a period of between one month and one year, the investor gets back the full value of the note. There is no shortage of investors. Those who have a few spare million dollars – often themselves cash rich corporations – believe that having certificates issued by companies like IBM, Ford or General Motors is as good a short term security as anything else, and if they want to get their money back before the IOU is payable there is a secondary market in which they can do this. In the United States the commercial paper market is worth over $300 billion, accounting for nearly one fifth of all private debt. By comparison the Eurocommercial paper market, usually denominated in dollars, is fledgling, but in 1986 alone over 50 companies used it to raise short-term capital. A more recent development has been a sterling commercial paper market, which, as its name implies, is for those companies, mostly British, that wish to raise funds in pounds.

Although the intention of commercial paper is as a vehicle to raise short term finance, many programmes are rolled over at the end of the life of the issue, with perhaps a new rate negotiated. Some commercial paper issues offer the possibility of converting the paper to equity at the expiry of the note. This is a cheap way of making a share issue, and it enables the company to tap international institutions without resorting to the normal procedures, and by-passing the stockmarkets.

International Equity Markets

The London Stock Exchange was not oblivious to these developments, but could see very little it could do about it; after all the growing commercial paper market was more of a threat to banks' blue chip loan business than to the sharemarkets.

Also, by the mid-eighties, it was faced with a much more serious problem – the development of an international equities market in London which by-passed the Stock Exchange altogether.

By 1984, 62 per cent of the trading in one of Britain's largest companies, ICI, was being transacted off the London Exchange, mainly in New York. A large share of the buying and selling of other major British companies has also been taking place in the United States. By the Stock Exchange's own estimates from a survey carried out during the last six months of 1984 there was heavy American trading in Reuters (50 per cent of total buying and selling), Glaxo (48 per cent), British Telecom (28 per cent), BP (20 per cent), Fisons (19 per cent), Shell Transport and Trading (16 per cent), Bowater (13 per cent) and Beecham (10 per cent). This trading has by no means been confined to American investors, for some of the big British institutions found that dealing across the Atlantic was a better proposition. Mick Newman, head of portfolio at the Prudential Assurance Company explained; 'When we have a significant buying programme on we check all available markets. We take the attitude that we deal wherever we can get the best price.'

In other words the big traders saw no need to deal in London, where the complicated system of brokers and jobbers was costing them much more in commission, government stamp duty and Value Added Tax. All this could be avoided by going through one of the large American brokers that run a 24-hour book – which means trade – in the stocks of major multinationals. This works by a dealer in major British stocks based in London handing his book over to a colleague in New York in mid-afternoon, who runs it for eight hours before passing it to a third colleague in Tokyo, who eight hours later passes it back to London again. Prices are governed by what buyers and sellers are prepared to pay, large blocks being sold at heavy discounts. At the time of writing, Goldman Sachs, one of the biggest traders in New York, operates a global market in 150 major stocks, 30 of which are British.

Since the great bulk of trade is in the major stocks, such competition posed a serious threat to an organization as rigid as the London Stock Exchange. Threatened with losing the massive institutional trading in major stocks, it was in danger of becoming just a sideshow for those British investors with an interest in lesser companies that form the second tier of equities. Lord Camoys, chief executive of London's largest new conglomerate, put it thus:

> London has been losing ground in securities dealing not only because of the way it organized its business, but also because the market's capital resources were rapidly becoming insufficient to meet changing circumstances. Preservation of the old system would have handed London's business on a plate to a new breed of dealers in world capital markets, such as Goldman Sachs, Merrill Lynch and Nomura Securities, as well as to banks like Citibank and Deutsche Bank.
>
> Investors in securities have looked increasingly across national borders to spread their risks. Thus, if the UK Government continues to tax the purchase of shares on the London Stock Exchange, investors now have the option of buying them in New York. If the German Government restricts Eurodeutschemark issues, European companies may choose to denominate bonds in ECUs, which are only 30 per cent D-Mark. If the United States Government prevents commercial banks from investment banking at home, they will overcome that by showing what they can do in the offshore markets through their subsidiaries in Britain, or elsewhere.

So, for Sir Nicholas Goodison, chairman of the Stock Exchange and his colleagues on the Council, sweeping reform was the only answer. If the Stock Exchange was to compete with the giant American broking houses, it had to join them at their own game. There was no choice, where competition was creaming off the top business, both in value and volume. Otherwise there would be nothing left for the old-fashioned Stock Exchange, and the jobbers would be left standing at their pitches.

The Big Bang

Effecting the necessary changes took time and considerable resolution. It meant ending a way of life that had been a tradition for more than 100 years. It meant abolishing a system that had secured a good income for thousands of people working for stockbrokers.

Even though its members saw the system was under threat, the Stock Exchange Council had to be given a firm nudge in the direction of change by the Government. This happened almost by accident. The Office of Fair Trading had argued that stockbrokers should be treated no differently from other sectors of the community – solicitors, estate agents, motor traders, soap powder manufacturers – who had been barred from fixing prices amongst each other, and were now bound to offer some semblance of competition in the market place. When the Stock Exchange demurred, the Government decided to take legal action, using the weight of the Monopolies Commission to take apart the entire rule book of the Exchange as a litany of restrictive practices. The proceedings were estimated to take five years to complete, and to cost at least £5m. in legal fees. It was, of course, using a sledgehammer to crack a nut and an absurd way of challenging an entire trading system. As Sir Nicholas Goodison was to say later;

> It was a foolish way to study the future of a great international market. It was a matter which needed long and close study, and preferably a public examination not constrained by the requirements of litigation or the straitjacket of court procedure. Unfortunately the Government turned down the suggestion of such an examination, and we were forced into a position of defence of rules, not all of which we would necessarily wish to

keep. This open debate became impossible because anything said could, as it were, be taken down in evidence and used in court. The case preempted resources, effort and thought.

It did, however, concentrate the mind of the Stock Exchange Council. The Government was clearly in no mood to set up a Royal Commission to inquire into the Stock Exchange; ministers saw that as a waste of time. If the case went on, with each side producing volumes of written evidence, as well as witnesses for examination, cross-examination and re-examination, the Stock exchange would end up in an unwinnable situation. There would also be unfavourable publicity. And even if the Exchange won, their joy would be shortlived, for such was the resolve of the Thatcher Government to curb the restrictive power of trades unions that it could hardly spare as notorious a City club as the Stock Exchange, and would then feel obliged to legislate to change the law.

In July 1983 the Government offered Sir Nicholas Goodison a way out. It offered to drop the case against the Stock Exchange, if the Council would abandon fixed commissions. It did so, and the die was cast for the Big Bang.

Both the Government and the Stock Exchange knew that the abolition of fixed commissions would be the catalyst for major change, for without steady reliance on a solid income, more or less indexed to the rate of inflation, many stockbrokers could not exist. Competition over commissions might be acceptable in a bull market, but when the bears emerged in strength there would be trouble. A bull is the name for the optimist who believes that prices are likely to go higher, and who charges into the market to buy; if there are enough bulls, their confidence is sufficient to push up prices. A bear is the opposite market animal, who fears the worst, and expects a fall; when the bears run for cover, you have a bear market. For stockbrokers, a bear market generates fear, for although there are good commissions to be had when there is pronounced selling, the prices on which those commissions are based are lower, and interest dies.

An end to fixed commissions altogether would mean a change in the way of life for most brokers, and the Old Guard did not like it. Life was cosy on a fixed commission.

Costs had gone up, but so had the rate of commission. In 1950 the commission on the purchase or sale of ordinary shares had been a sliding scale falling to 0.5 per cent for larger trades. According to Messrs Basil, Montgomery, Lloyd and Ward's pocket guide, a share valued at 15s. (at the old rate of 20 shillings to the pound and 12 pence to a shilling) then would cost the investor 15s. 5¼d., after paying stamp duty of 3¾d. and commission of 1½d. A £5 share would cost £5 2s. 9d., with the broker getting 9d. for his pains. By 1952 commission rates had gone up – to 0.75 per cent for large trades, but the 15s. share still cost the investor only ¾d. more at 15s. 6d., while the £5 share cost him £5 3s., with the broker getting a whole shilling instead of 9d. for the trade. Ten years later the rates were much higher at 1.25 per cent, but in the case of transactions of over £2,500, the broker could, at his descretion, reduce the commission for the surplus to not less than half the standard rate, provided the business was not shared with an agent, in which case the full rate had to be charged. On 24 February 1975 there was another rise – to 1.5 per cent for the first £5,000 consideration, falling to 0.625 per cent for the next £15,000. Decimalization had made calculations simpler; the £5 share now cost the investor £5.1625, of which 10p. went in stamp duty and 6.25p. in commission.

On this rate the average broker did not even have to worry overmuch about share prices, because, as we shall see later, jobbers fixed them, and took the risk. There was no need to worry overmuch about losing business to competitors, because there was just about enough to go round, and advertising was banned. You obtained clients through 'connections' and some wining and dining. There was no serious worry about finding and keeping staff because, in the clublike atmosphere of the Stock Exchange, loyalties to individual firms were high. There was little danger to health from overwork. Client interest in shares in North America and the Pacific Basin had extended the working day a little, so an early start was desirable, with a partners' meeting at 8.30, and of course it was no longer possible to catch the 4.48 train home to the stockbroker belt, a group of leafy suburbs in Surrey or Kent. But a good lunch with clients in a private dining room was a compensation, and the weekends could be spent on the golfcourse.

Under the 'Big Bang', the Old Guard knew, everything would be very different. Those who wanted to survive would have to behave like Chicago futures dealers. Life would become just like a job on the money or commodity markets, where young men and women would arrive to a room full of telephones and computer terminals at 7.30 every morning, scream at them and at each other for at least 12 hours, and leave exhausted in the evening. This was a world where the mid-life crisis came at the age of 26.

And competition would be so fierce there would probably be less money in it anyway. With no fixed commissions, firms would have neither the time nor the resources to undertake company or sector research, let alone visit a firm and enjoy a steak and kidney pie in a country hotel with the chairman and managing director. Instead they would spend their days peering at monitors, and bawling down the telephone.

As for open ownership, well, the senior partners would sell out, pocket their millions, and go and live in Bermuda, whilst those left would not know who their bosses were, only that they worked for some large bank, almost certainly under foreign ownership.

All Change at the Stock Exchange

The crucial vote

Despite their defeat over commissions, the Old Guard held out against other reforms. However on 4 June 1985 the 4,495 members of the Stock Exchange were confronted with an historic choice: to face up to the future or face the consequences of living with the past.

Two resolutions were put to the members' vote on the floor of the Exchange. For Sir Nicholas Goodison, the issue was clear. It was about 'whether or not members want to keep the bulk of the securities business in this country and in the Stock Exchange', he wrote in a letter. 'It is about keeping and strengthening the Stock Exchange as the natural market in securities.'

The first resolution, which required only a simple majority, would enable outsiders – banks, mining finance houses, international conglomerates, money brokers – to own up to 100 per cent of a member firm, instead of only 29.9 per cent. The second resolution required a 75 per cent majority, and proposed changes in the Stock Exchange Constitution to shift ownership of the Exchange from individual members to member firms. Plans were to be devised whereby members could sell their shares in the Exchange to newcomers.

The first resolution was passed by 3,246 votes to 681, but the second failed by a very small margin to achieve the required majority, achieving 73.64 per cent instead of the required 75 per cent. For Goodison, this was a major setback, but for those who had voted against it, it was to prove an even greater blow.

Goodison had already warned members that to reject the proposal would be 'very serious and could cause substantial damage to the standing of the Stock Exchange', mainly because new entrants from America and elsewhere, if denied easy membership, would decide simply to by-pass its activities. But Goodison had one major card to play. Under his leadership the Stock Exchange's reputation and credibility have been high. In almost every other area of the City there has been scandal, but the Stock Exchange has retained its integrity, and has been shown to be a far more effective policeman of those within its province than the Bank of England. Goodison was able to secure the Stock Exchange's right to self-regulation under the Conservative Government's proposed financial services legislation, thus making it certain that those who wished to trade in British equities would want to be governed by its rules. The Exchange's Council then moved to create the new class of corporate membership, effective from March 1986.

Corporate members can each own one share, which gives them the right to take part in all of the Stock Exchange's trading activities, and to use its settlement and other facilities. But there is no need for any corporate member to have an individual member on either its board or staff, although all those in its employ who have contact with customers must be 'approved persons'. Thus those members who had voted against the Council on the second resolution in the hope of getting better terms for selling their individual shares to new conglomerate members found that these shares were virtually worthless. The biggest group in the world could join the club for only one share, negotiating the price, not with old members, but with the Stock Exchange Council.

The Stock Exchange retains the right to discipline individuals in the new conglomerates, however, even though these individuals are not members. But Goodison did have to make one major concession. Up to March 1986 all members had to take the Stock Exchange examinations. This has had to be waived for those working for corporate members, mainly because most of the experienced staff coming under the aegis of the Exchange would be unwilling to take the examinations.

The world's first international exchange

No sooner had the new deal gone through and the day of 'Big Bang' passed, relatively without incident, than Goodison achieved a major coup. As outlined earlier, one of the major threats to the London Stock Exchange was international equity trading, by-passing London altogether. Even though the new rules made London less uncompetitive – and electronic dealing systems forced traders to work faster – there was still a large group of securities houses trading international stocks who saw no good reason why they should be part of the new Exchange.

They had formed themselves into ISRO, the International Securities Regulatory Organization, which, despite its grandiose title, showed very little affection for regulation. Its members traded in the stocks of about 400 of the world's major corporations for the benefit of about 80 institutions. It was an exclusive club for the big boys, who argued that since they all knew each other not many rules were needed.

Prior to 'Big Bang' ISRO and the London Exchange were not exactly the best of friends; indeed they often traded insults. Since international equities were stocks which were traded beyond their own country boundaries, it was argued they should not be subject to rigid domestic rules. And a new class of international equity was being spawned; issues by international corporations underwritten and distributed in alien countries. The first really large issue of this kind was British Telecom; when it was floated off by the British

Government a large proportion of the stock was successfully offered to institutions in North America, Europe and Japan.

Such international equity issues are organized by merchant banks and securities houses who offer tranches of stock directly to favoured clients without touching the stock markets. Because of London's position at the centre of the world business time zone, most of this business has been conducted in there. Goodison approached ISRO and suggested that sooner or later some form of ordered regulation for the conduct of global equity markets would be forced on it if it did not form an international standard of its own; and since the London Stock Exchange offered the nearest to such a standard, why not merge with it?

From the Stock Exchange point of view the proposed deal averted the possibility of the world's financial giants setting up a competing marketplace in London, and, according to Goodison, opened 'the way for a united securities market which will be a very powerful competitor for international business'.

On November 12 1986, members of the Stock Exchange voted for the merger, and the combined body became known as the International Stock Exchange of the United Kingdom and Northern Ireland. The old guard knew there was no choice – the new Exchange was going to be dominated by foreigners, but so what? The previous changes they had approved had already allowed foreign financial houses to take over two-thirds of British broking firms, and so domination by the likes of Citicorp, American Express, Deutschebank, Merrill Lynch, Nomura, and the Swiss Banking Corporation was anyway inevitable. There was also a sweetener of £10,000 for each member when they retire or reach the age of 60.

The new conglomerates

The establishment of giant new conglomerates led to an undignified scramble as City and international broking firms, banks and finance houses rushed to jump into bed with each other. So unseemly was the haste that some parted company with new-found, if expensive, friends within days rather than weeks, in a kind of financial promiscuity which must have left old faithfuls gasping for breath. One major bank bought a firm of jobbers only to find that, by the time the ink was dry on the contract, the best people had all left en masse to join a rival. Since these people had been almost the firm's only asset, the acquisition was more or less worthless. The Deputy Governor of the Bank of England put his finger on the problem:

> If key staff – and on occasions whole teams – can be offered inducements to move suddenly from one institution to another, it becomes very difficult for any bank to rely on the commitment individuals will give to implementing its plans, and adds a further dimension of risk to any bank which is building its strategy largely around a few individuals' skills.

The banks and merchant banks were the predators, but they found even the very large broking forms only too willing to submit. Typical of the alliances formed was Barclays De Zoete Wedd, a merger between the investing banking side of Barclays Bank plc, the large stockbrokers De Zoete and Bevan, and London's largest stockjobber in gilt-edged securities, Wedd, Durlacher & Mordaunt. Barclays became top dog, owning 75 per cent of the shares. Another group is Mercury, formed by S. G. Warburg and Co., with three major broking and jobbing firms. Each of these two giants is able to issue securities, to place them with its large clientele base, and to buy and sell speculatively on its own account. Each has capital of about £300m., compared with the total capital capacity of about £100m. of the entire old London stockjobbing community. This makes them sound big and they are big, by traditional London standards. But compared with Japan's Nomura Securities, with capital of over US$35.7bn., and New York's Merrill Lynch, with resources of over $3bn., they are minnows.

All but one of Britain's top twenty broking and jobbing houses have been absorbed into large new financial conglomerates. Among the leading firms, only Cazenove and Co. remains independent and has declared its determination to do so. By taking this step, it may expect to benefit from both institutions and private investors seeking out brokers with no commercial link, and therefore no potential conflict of interest, with a bank, an insurance company, or a unit trust management company.

The aim of the majority which did make arrangements for conglomerates was extensively publicized. Barclays De Zoete Wedd described its tripartite partnership as 'strategically defensive and offensive'. 'Barclays' decision to enter the fray was made both to protect and retain, as well as to consolidate and expand our business,' said Lord Camoys. Though a laudable aim in many ways, this is the very point that most concerned the Stock Exchange traditionalists. What would happen, they asked, when BZW used its clout to grab all the business? And what about conflict of interest? When Warburgs, to take another example, was advising a company involved in a takeover, would this proscribe integrated partners like Ackroyd and Co., Rowe and Pitman, and Mullens and Co. from dealing in the company's shares? So far branches of the same company have shown remarkable independence; for example BZW advised its clients to sell their shares in Barclays Bank, its parents.

Yet the City has spawned new monoliths which can, in parallel, act as bankers to a company, raise long-term debt or equity, make a market in its shares, retail them to investors, and buy them as managers of discretionary funds. How can the public be sure that those at the marketing end of the firm are not privy to insider information, and, if they are, how can they be prevented from acting upon it? Sensitive information does not, of course, have to be in written form in a report; a nudge and a wink over lunch is a more subtle, more common, and less detectable way of passing secrets. The official Stock Exchange answer to this problem, to be discussed in greater depth in Chapter 9, is that 'Chinese Walls' must be erected between the various parts of a financial services company, so that the interest of the public or investors comes first.

The arrival of the new monoliths also upset the staid city career structure. Salaries rocketed as a game of musical chairs for all but the most mundane jobs got under way. Staffs of merchant banks and broking firms, whose only regular bright spot had previously been the annual bonus payment, suddenly found, to their wonderment, that they had taken over from soccer professionals as the group in society most likely to be able to bid up earnings without lifting their game. 'The trick,' one 26-year-old woman employed by a Swiss bank told me, 'is to always appear to be in demand. If they think you are about to leave, they will offer more without you having to ask for it.'

The taxmen in thc City District must be bemused by the sudden windfall of intelligence as well as potential revenue, when salaries appeared in print as well as in bar gossip. In the City's wine bars in 1986 the talk was of golden handshakes, golden hellos, parachutes, and honeypots, and of how the place to be is the 'marzipan layer' or 'the froth' – in other words just below the top. The following story, credited to Margareta Pagano of *The Guardian* is by no means untypical:

> A few weeks ago a young Eurobond dealer in the City of London, with two years' experience, was tempted away by a rival firm for a salary of £30,000. Before the 25-year-old had time to quit, he received another approach – this time for £45,000. He quickly seized the chance, but within days there came yet another call, offering to snatch him away for £70,000. The young dealer, one of a new wave of graduates, seduced by the prospect of a quick buck in the City told the headhunter not to bother him in future with offers less than £100,000.

Those of us toiling for more modest incomes had to comfort ourselves in the knowledge that when a similar madhouse was induced in New York's own Big Bang several years ago, there was a short burst of excitement, and then a massive shakeout. It seems certain that the City will follow the same route.

Fast money

But that is for the future. Along with a move towards a super league of financial conglomerates came another major switch of attitudes – an obsession with short-term performance.

It has become clear that fund managers – the men and women who manage the money in pension funds, life assurance companies and unit trusts – are no longer prepared to play safe by maintaining large holdings in giant but dull corporations. Not long ago the average institutional investor shared his portfolio between government gilt-edged securities (interest-bearing bonds) and blue-chip equities (shares in well-known companies like Unilever, BP and ICI).

Now they prefer to move their money around, terrifying

corporate treasurers who watch, helpless, as large blocks of their companies' shares are traded for what seems fashion or a whim. A fund manager may desert GEC, as many did in 1985, and buy into Siemens of Germany, ASEA of Sweden, or Sony of Japan, thereby gambling on future currency movements as well as on the future profitability of a company or market sector. Or he may buy Eurobonds. And because of the risk of volatile movements in exchange or interest rates, he may protect himself by an options or futures contract (of which more later), or both.

The upshot of this is that fund managers tend towards taking profits whenever they present themselves, which in the bull market which London has enjoyed for more than a decade, is often. Turnover on the stock markets has remained high, which keeps the brokers happy.

But there is the other consequence, of course, that the companies whose financial performances are, at best, languid cease to have the wholesale support of the institutions, and their share prices fall, making them ripe for takeover. It is no coincidence that Britain has just witnessed a wave of takeover fever, as aggressive, cash-rich – and not-so-rich – predators try to buy useful capital assets on the cheap.

The run-up to Christmas is normally a quiet period in the City, as brokers ponder and pull to pieces each other's end-of-year forecasts. Christmas 1985, with about £10bn. of takeover money in the wind, was an exception. The late-night calm of the Square Mile was nightly broken by the unmistakable rattle of taxi-cabs, as letters and offer documents were ferried to and from the offices of merchant banks. 'I have never known anything like it,' one cabbie told me cheerfully. 'It beats hanging around the Savoy.' 'These people insist on having meetings on a Sunday,' wailed a man from Warburg's. 'This will be the third weekend in a row I have lost.'

Major bids during those weeks included GEC's £1.16bn. bid for Plessey, Argyll Group's £1.9bn. offer for Distillers, a £1.5bn. merger between Habitat and British Home Stores, a £217m. offer by Guinness Peat for Britannia Arrow, and a £2bn. bid by Hanson Trust for the Imperial Group, itself in merger talks with United Biscuits. These followed successful takeovers of Harrods by the Al-Fayed brothers, of

Debenhams by the Burton Group, and of Bell's whisky by Guinness.

The savings mountain

The other unexpected development has been that in the 1970s and 1980s the British people, perhaps unwittingly, have become a nation of savers, so that the City has much more cash to play with. This does not mean that we all have more on deposit in the bank or building society, but that more people have more money locked up in long-term savings through life assurance and pension schemes. Cash flow in these institutions has risen from £5.4bn. in 1976 to over £18bn. in 1985, a reflection both of a growing awareness of the need to plan for retirement and of a better performance by fund managers who, since the abolition of exchange controls, have had the freedom to invest wherever they wish.

Interest in the City has also been fuelled by the Government's privatization programme. While there is no evidence that this in any way affects the dominance of the large institutions on the market, it does mean that there are millions more individual shareholders in Britain.

A Clean Place to do Business?

The changes in the City will mean different things to different people, but the fact that some old established forms will go to the wall, that some overgilded executives will face the chop, and that many restrictive practices will fade away is of only minor concern. Manufacturing industry has been through just such a harrowing process, and the new efficiencies being introduced to the Square Mile are only a long overdue repetition of what has happened elsewhere.

For the public only one thing really matters. Will the City be a clean place in which to do business? Can the City be trusted? *The Financial Times* raised this crucial issue in an admirable editorial on 19 December 1985, following the introduction of the Financial Services Bill in the House of Commons:

The City of London stands at a lower point in the public's

> esteem than it has for many years. Standards of behaviour in the financial markets have slipped to the point where transactions which used to be undertaken on trust now have to be scrutinized by teams of lawyers.

The Financial Times also listed as a priority the need for the 'old City clubs to be finally opened to full scrutiny'.

> The Stock Exchange Council has come a long way, but by comparison with the ruling body of the New York Stock Exchange – which is run on the lines of a public company – it still looks Victorian.

Improved service?

There are other important questions. Will all this change benefit the consumer, meaning, in this instance, both the small investor and the large institutions managing the people's savings and their pension funds? If not, what is the reason for making it?

There is, as yet, no evidence at all that the standard of service from financial groups has improved, nor is there any real hope that it will. As is often the case with radical change, expectations were high at the outset, but they were progressively lowered as the first day of the Stock Exchange new order approached, and passed.

Even *The Economist*, often at the forefront of radical proposals for altering the management of the economy, was doubtful whether the Big Bank would be of lasting benefit. Rather, in a 1985 report *All Change in the City* it stated that the fierce competition which financial groups faced would encourage them to take on more risky business in banking, as well as encouraging unnecessary trading in securities.

> The form of organization of financial firms that is being most actively created, the conglomerate, will promote bad business. These firms will be increasingly reluctant to refuse, for instance, loans to less than fully creditworthy customers for fear of losing any other, albeit sound, business that they have with them.

Nor did it believe that those who had pushed the change through had a clear picture of the new environment they were creating.

> Those in the Treasury, Bank of England and the Department of

Trade and Industry are inspired by vague and superficial notions of competition and enterprise that have little relevance to the situation of finance in a sophisticated and industrialized market economy.

The flight of money

There are also doubts that City money will benefit the rest of the country. It would be good to think that a proportion of the huge volume of funds flowing into London would find its way into some of the most badly neglected areas of Britain, such as the faded cities of Birmingham, Liverpool and Newcastle, or the depressed regions of the North, Wales, Scotland and Northern Ireland.

But this is a false hope, for even the money raised by British institutions from savers in the United Kingdom is likely to fuel investments outside this country. In the months of April, May and June 1985, £1.17bn. of British savings – in pension funds, life assurance companies, building societies and investment trusts – found its way into overseas equities. It was the largest ever outflow in one quarter, and compared with only £46m. leaving the country in the whole of the previous year.

The overseas portfolio of the British non-bank private sector rose from £11bn. at the end of 1979, the year when exchange controls were ended, to an estimated £63bn. at the end of 1984. Of this £63bn., £21.2bn. had been placed by British pension funds, £14bn. by insurance funds, and over £12bn. by unit trusts and investment trusts. By contrast portfolio investment coming into Britain was a mere trickle – £2.5bn. in the four years to the end of 1984. The figures have not improved since then. Those who manage large British funds have a taste for foreign stocks, and like to hold about 20 per cent of their portfolio in non-British stocks. They can, and do, contend that it is their right and their duty to do so. We have a free market economy, and the days of exchange controls are happily long past. The fund manager is right to see his job as getting the best investment value for each pound in his care. In economic terms, the capital outflows have prevented sterling from rising more strongly through the benefits of North Sea oil; without overseas investment, its strength would have brought even more serious problems for manufactured exports.

Unfortunately socialist politicians do not share this view, and argue strongly for the direction of investment to what they believe to be worthwhile (British) enterprise. Present Labour Party policy is to discourage those who invest overseas through penal taxation. I suspect that few middle-of-the-road voters – the ones that decide an election – support such a policy, and, in economic terms, it would be an inefficient way of raising tax revenues.

It is, however, possible to reject Labour's dogmatic policy but at the same time to feel unease at the indifference displayed by the City towards anything north of Watford. The yawning culture and wealth gap between London and provincial Britain is likely to get much worse as salaries, rents and costs in the City rise sharply compared with elsewhere. While the City revolution will provide a magnet for young people, it could bring bitter results elsewhere. What must a college-trained and unemployed process engineer feel when he reads that a 21-year-old bond dealer is earning £50,000 a year? To be sure, the City needs freedom from excessive regulations and independence, but it is to be hoped that it does not become so engrossed in its own self-enrichment as to ignore the other Britain still facing a desperate economic struggle to survive. It will do so at its peril.

Good Advice and Bad Advice

The problems of avarice in the City, the flight of capital overseas, and poor service may prove to be of much less consequence to the average British family than the worries over investor protection. Acknowledging that savers and investors may need protection against themselves, the Government wisely decided in 1986 that the old maxim of *caveat emptor* could not be applied to the financial services industry. Unfortunately its legislation is a classic British fudge – an uneasy compromise between the American notion of a Securities and Exchange Commission and a system of voluntary controls.

City men say that it is reputation that is all-important, and that the best financial conglomerates will be most anxious to build and maintain credibility with the public. With the ring of major scandals in our ears this is just a joke. It's also not the point. It never ceases to amaze me that normally-prudent breadwinners will fill in coupons from advertisements in journals purporting to offer investment advice, enclosing with them cheques for hundreds or even thousands of pounds. Many of these people have scant knowledge of their proposed investment, and even less idea of how much they are being charged in fees. It is important that such people should be protected.

The new system, discussed in detail later, goes some way towards meeting the need for adequate protection in a flexible market place, but the raw investor is still at the mercy of the more predatory sharks in the City. By far the most serious worry is that all these changes will lead to enormous and irreconcilable conflicts of interest. This is not new to the City. But in the days when banks stuck to banking, brokers to brokerage, financial advisers to advising, and insurers to insurance, things were much easier to control.

2 History

'Dictum meum pactum, My word is my bond.' The Stock Exchange Handbook.

'The want of a written contract between members had in practice no evil results, and out of the millions of contracts made on the Stock Exchange, such a thing was hardly known as a dispute as to the existence of a contact or as to its terms'. Report of the Commissioners of the London Stock Exchange Commission, 1878.

From the controversy that prefaced the publication of the Financial Services Bill on 19 December 1985 one might have thought that it was the first Act of Parliament to regulate the activities of the Stock Exchange. This is not the case. After a wave of market-rigging and insider trading, the Government as long ago as 1697 brought in an Act designed 'to restrain the number and ill-practice of brokers and stock-jobbers'. This followed a report from a Parliamentary Commission set up a year earlier which had discovered that:

> the pernicious art of stockjobbing hath, of late, so perverted the end design of Companies and Corporations, erected for the introducing or carrying on of manufactures, to the private profit of the first projectors, that the privileges granted to them have commonly been made no other use of – but to sell again, with advantage, to innocent men.

As a result of the 1697 Act all stockbrokers and stockjobbers had to be licensed before they plied their trade in the coffee shops, walks and alleys near the Royal Exchange. These licences were limited to 100 and were granted by the Lord Mayor of London and the Court of Aldermen. They cost only £2, and entitled the licensee to wear a specially struck silver medal embossed with the Royal Arms, once he had taken an oath that he would 'truly and faithfully execute and perform the office and employment of a broker between party and party, without fraud or collusion'.

The rules of operation were strict. Brokers were not allowed to deal on their own behalf, but only for clients. They could not hold any options for more than three days without facing the certainty of permanent expulsion. Commission was limited to 5 per cent, or less. Anyone who tried to operate as a broker without a licence was, if caught, exposed to three days in the City pillory.

Muscovy and Company

The trade in shares had started with City traders and merchants spreading the risk of two major entrepreneurial journeys: an attempt to investigate the prospects offered by the uncharted White Sea and Arctic Circle, and a voyage to India and the East Indies via the Cape of Good Hope. These ventures were to lead to the first two public companies: the Muscovy Company and the East India Company, whose members did not follow previous practice of trading on their own account, but contributed money to 'joint stock', through shares which were freely transferable.

The Muscovy Company emerged from a brave, if unsuccessful attempt by Sebastian Cabot in 1553 to find a North East trade route to China and the Orient. As one of the first shareholders explained at the time:

> Every man willing to bee of the societie, should disburse the portion of twentie and five pounds a piece: so that in a short time, by this means, the sum of six thousand pounds being gathered, three ships were brought.

The East India Company was more successful and was the first to raise equity capital on a substantial scale. It needed modern, armed ships for the difficult and dangerous voyage to the Orient, and substantial docks in London. Although it lost ships on voyages, and hovered close to bankruptcy, it managed to raise over £1.6m. in 17 years. As the silk and spice trade developed, those who had invested in the original stock saw profit returns of 40 per cent a year.

Enterprising developers quickly realized that raising capital through shares had potential far beyond risky voyages. Why not try it at home? Francis, Earl of Bedford had a bold plan to drain the Fens, which would provide more fertile agricultural land as well as giving London its first supply of fresh water. So others topped up his own £100,000 contribution and 'The Governor and Company of the New River brought from Chadwell and Amwell to London' was founded in 1609. Although the water company operations were bought out by the Metropolitan Water Board in 1904, the company still exists as the oldest one quoted on the Stock Exchange.

The Stock Exchange Official List

By the end of the seventeenth century there was substantial dealing in shares of one sort or another. It was estimated by the historian W. R. Scott that by 1695 there were some 140 joint stock companies, with a total market capitalization of £4.5m. More by habit than by design, much of this took place in two coffee houses called Garraway's and Jonathan's near Change Alley, which still exists in the narrow spit of land between Cornhill and Threadneedle Street. The coffee establishments of the seventeenth century had style. You could meet there fellow merchants and traders, discuss the latest ventures, and buy and sell shares. You could also run your eye down a sheet of paper containing prices of commodities and a few shares – called 'The Course of the Exchange and Other Things'; this was to be the precursor of the Stock Exchange Daily Official List.

A writer of the day set the scene:

> The centre of the jobbing is in the Kingdom of Exchange Alley and its adjacencies: the limits are easily surrounded in about a Minute and a half stepping out of Jonathan's into the Alley, you turn your face full South, moving on a few paces, and then turning Due East, you advance to Garaway's; from there going out at the other Door, you go on still East into Birchin Lane and then halting a little at the Sword-Blade Bank to do much mischief in fervent Words, you immediately face to the North, enter Cornhill, visit two or three petty Provinces there in your way West; and thus having Boxed your Compass, and sail'd

round the whole Stock Jobbing Globe, you turn into Jonathan's again; and so, as most of the great Follies of Life oblige us to do, you end just where you began.

South Sea Bubble

This coffee society was to thrive for more than 50 years, and by 1720 Change Alley, and its coffee houses thronged with brokers, was the place to be. The narrow streets were impassable because of the throng of lords and ladies in their carriages. The Act regulating and restricting their operations had lapsed, by popular consent. And the eighteenth-century equivalent of the hit parade contained the following ballad:

Then stars and garters did appear
Among the meaner rabble
To buy and sell, to see and hear
The Jews and Gentiles squabble,
The greatest ladies thither came
And plied in chariots daily,
Or pawned their jewels for a sum
To venture in the Alley.

The principal attraction was the excitement caused by the booming share prices of the South Sea Company, which started in 1720 at £128 apiece, and swiftly rose as euphoria about their prospects was spread both by brokers and by the Government. By March the price rose to £330, by May it was £550, and by 24 June it had reached an insane £1,050.

The South Sea Company had been set up nine years earlier by the British Government ostensibly with the aim of opening up trade and markets for new commodities in South America. It also had another purpose, which, these days, has a familiar ring about it, for it was to relieve the Government of some £9m. of public debt.

For eight years it did virtually nothing, and created no excitement. Its shares were static, and it had only one contract of any size, to supply black slaves to Latin America. The Government then gave birth to the concept of privatization of a State concern and one much more audacious then the current sales of British Telecom or British Gas. It offered shares in the South Sea Company to the public, hoping that it would raise enough money to wipe out the entire National Debt of some £31m.

The Government was persuaded to do this by a wily operator, Sir John Blunt, who was a director of the company and effectively underwrote the issue. The issues were 'partly-paid'; an investor had to find only a small proportion at the start, and then pay the rest of the share price in instalments. (Where have you heard this before?) The issue was heavily oversubscribed, and there was much irritation when it was discovered that Blunt's acquaintances, and others of influence, had received an extra allocation (another familiar tale). To raise still more money, the company made loans to the public secured on the shares themselves, provided the money was used to buy more stock. Blunt also proved adept at the use of public relations in pushing the share price up. There were promises of lavish dividends, the interest of prominent people was secured by thinly veiled bribes, and the peace negotiations with Spain were used for propaganda purposes, for the prospect of an end to conflict meant more trade with South America.

The smart money, including the Prime Minister, Sir Robert Walpole, sold out at the peak of the boom. The Prince of Wales, the Duke of Argyll, the Chancellor of the Exchequer and MPs too numerous to mention made handsome gains before the bubble burst, when the Government, by bringing in the Bubble Act designed to prevent a rash of similar, and competitive, enterprises from springing up, triggered off the first ever bear market. But the bubble did burst, and within eight weeks of passing £1,000, the share price had plunged to £175. By December it had sunk to £124, bringing ruin to those who had seen the South Sea Company as the chance of a lifetime. There was the inevitable Parliamentary inquiry, which concluded that the accounts had been falsified and government minister bribed. The Chancellor had no chance to enjoy his £800,000 capital gain; he was committed to the Tower after being found guilty of the 'most notorious, dangerous and infamous corruption'.

It was – and remains – the most notorious episode in British financial history, and it was a long time before the market got back into its stride. Indeed it was not until the next century that a large crop of joint stock companies were formed, a development brought about by an acute shortage of capital for major projects both at home and abroad.

Mines, Railways, Canals

By 1824, the end of the cyclical trade depression, there were 156 companies quoted on the London Stock Exchange, with a market capitalization of £47.9m. In the following twelve months interest in investment increased sharply. Prospectuses were issued for no less than 624 companies with capital requirements of £372m. The largest group were general investment companies, mostly with extensive interests overseas, which raised £52m. Canals and railways came next, raising £44m., followed by mining companies, £38m. and insurance, a new industry, with £35m.

The railways proved a great boon for the promotion of investment, even if most of the investors lost their shirts. The Duke of Wellington had opposed the development of railways; 'railroads will only encourage the lower classes to move about needlessly'. Not only did this prove to be the case, but investment in the railways also led to the spread of share ownership outside London and the ruling classes to the provinces. It also created a new word in the financial vocabulary: stag, a person who applied for an allotment of shares with the clear intention of selling them to someone else before he has to pay for them.

The stags were out in force in 1836 when George Hudson, a bluff Yorkshireman, raised £300,000 for the York and North Midland Railway under the slogan 'Mak' all t'railways coom t'York'. The £50 shares were oversubscribed, and quickly gained a premium of £4 each. Within three years, the line was opened, and the bells of York Minster pealed out in joyful celebration. Much of the joy was short-lived, however, for so many railway lines sprouted up across the country that many of them could not pay the wages of the train drivers, let alone dividends. Many of them also turned out to be overcapitalized, with the surplus funds vanishing into other ventures, to the shareholders' chagrin.

Even so, despite setbacks, by 1842 there were 66 railway companies quoted on the London Stock Exchange, with a capital of almost £50m. During the boom in railway issues, *The Economist* was moved to write an editorial, which, with a change of name and date, might well have fitted into the British Telecom era of 1985. 'Everybody is in the stocks now (sic),' it purred. 'Needy clerks, poor tradesmen's apprentices, discarded serving men, and bankrupts – all have entered the ranks of the great moneyed interest.'

Provincial stock markets were also being established. Local investment opportunities had been featured in the advertisements of share auctions which regularly appeared in the Liverpool newspapers after about 1827. It was quite usual to use a property auction as the opportunity to dispose of a parcel of shares. By the middle of 1845 regional stock exchanges had been formed in 12 towns and cities, from Bristol in the South to Newcastle in the North, with Yorkshire claiming the greatest number. But only five of them survived the trading slump of 1845 to become permanent institutions.

Government Debt

All through this period government debt had been growing, and its funding was providing the most lucrative and reliable form of income to sharebrokers. In 1860, British funds amounted to more than all the other quoted securities combined, and provided by far the widest market in the Exchange. Compensation to slave-owners, whose slaves had been freed, the cost of the Crimean War, and the purchase by the Government of the national telegraph system all added to the cost.

Government stocks, or bonds, were bought daily from the Treasury by the City figure called the Government broker, who then sold them on in the market-place. The idea was that these stocks, to become known much later as gilt-edged securities, would be used to cut back or even get rid of the National Debt. In effect, of course, they added to the debt, but they were a way of funding unpopular measures without resorting to excessive taxation. By the early twentieth century local authorities had also jumped on the bandwagon. The City of Dublin was the first to raise money through bonds, followed by Edinburgh, Glasgow and the Metropolitan Board of Works.

The First Exchange

The brokers and other money dealers had, of course, long since left their damp pitches in Change Alley, and the coffee shops had not only become too crowded but also too accommodating to groups which the more established professionals liked to call the 'riff-raff'. When Jonathan's was finally burnt down after a series of major fires around 1748, the broking industry sought refuge in New Jonathan's, rebuilt in Threadneedle Street, where they charged sixpence a day entrance fee, a sum sufficient to discourage tinkers, money-lenders and the other parasites that had frequented the previous premises. Soon afterwards they put a sign over the door: The Stock Exchange.

It continued in this way, more or less as a club, for 30 years, until its members decided something more formal was required. On 7 February 1801 its days as the Stock Exchange ended and it was shut down, to reopen one month later as the 'Stock Subscription Room'. It no longer cost sixpence a day to enter; members had to be elected and to pay a fee of ten guineas, and risk a fine of two guineas if they were found guilty of 'disorderly conduct', the penalty going to charity. There does not seem to be an accurate record of how much charities benefited from this provision. The Stock Subscription Room had a short life, for members quickly decided it was too small, and in the same year laid the foundation stone for a new building in Capel Court. The stone records that this was also the 'first year of the union between Great Britain and Ireland', and notes that the building was being 'erected by private subscription for transaction of the business in the public funds'.

Not all members of the public were impressed by this new monument; the old lady who sold cups of tea and sweet buns outside Capel Court moved away because, she said, 'the Stock Exchange is such a wicked place'. But with monuments come tablets, and it was not long before members were forced to draw up new rules of operation. Adopted in 1812, these still form the basis of the present-day rule book. Neither members nor their wives could be engaged in any other business, failures had to be chalked up above the clock immediately so that there could be a fair distribution of assets to creditors, and members were informed they had to give up 'rude and trifling practices which have long disgraced the Stock Exchange'.

The Capel Court building was to last a century and a half, and it was, in the end, not size but ancient communications that made it unworkable. The decision was taken to rebuild, and the present Stock Exchange now occupies a 321-feet high, 26-storey tower, which is one of the few high-rise buildings in the City that are both attractive and practical. There are especially good facilities for visitors; from a large first-floor gallery they can watch the proceedings at any time, without intruding on the business of the day. But these days, as we shall see later, very little business actually takes place on the floor.

3 How It Works

'There is nothing more difficult to take in hand, more perilous to conduct, more certain in its success, than to take the lead in introducing a new order of things; because the innovator will have for enemies all who have done well under the old conditions and only lukewarm defenders in those who may do well under the new' – Machiavelli, *The Prince*.

The buying and selling of shares is often compared with the trade in fresh vegetables, in an attempt to show how simple it is. The truth is that it is not simple at all, which is perhaps surprising, given that until 'Big Bang' in October 1986 most transactions took place in one large room, the floor of the London Stock Exchange, whereas boxes of apples pass through many middle-men and mark-ups between the time they are picked in a Kent orchard until, perhaps weeks later, they end up in someone's plastic carrier bag outside a suburban greengrocer's shop.

The difference is, of course, that apples are perishable, whereas shares, for the most part, are not. Title to shares is as important as title to real estate. The price and time at which shares are traded are also an essential matter of record, not only for the buyer and seller but also for any potential subsequent inquiry as to whether the deal struck was a fair one or arrived at as a result of a breach of the Stock Exchange rules, such as trading through inside knowledge not available to the ordinary investor or member of the public.

Now an investor can purchase shares from home through an electronic terminal. By means of a service like Prestel, he is able to review the very latest price of any share in which he is interested, and place an order through the firm offering the best deal. Already the Topic teletext facility offered by the Stock Exchange provides a constant service not only of the last price quoted for every share, but also the prices at which the leading stocks may be bought or sold.

All that is possible, but most people's share trading in fact differs little from the system that has been in operation throughout this century. They will telephone a stockbroker, or their bank, and place an order for the purchase of, say, 200 BP shares. When dealing with a broker, they will probably seek, or be given, advice, particularly about the price of the contemplated purchase. In the case of a bank, unless things change for the better as a result of bank entry into stockbroking, they will find themselves dealing with a clerk on the general inquiry counter who will invariably respond, if asked, that 'we'll buy at best', which, of course neatly removes the bank from any responsibility for buying too expensively, or, in the case of a sale, of selling too cheap, although the customer can always specify a limit. The buyer's broker, or the buyer's bank's broker, should then immediately pass the order to one of the firm's recognized dealers. It is at this point that the new arrangements differ substantially from the old. It may be helpful if I describe both the old system, applicable until the autumn of 1986, and the new.

The Jobbers' Pitch

Under the old system, the dealer, armed with the order, or several orders, made his way to one of several pitches, or stalls, specializing in the sector in which he had been asked to buy – in this example oils. Here he encountered the Stock Exchange's barrow boy, the stockjobber, who either sat on a slightly elevated bench, or, more often, stood close by, surrounded by a sea of paper, much like a stall trader at the end of market day.

Without disclosing whether he was a potential buyer or seller, the dealer would seek a quote on BP's price. The jobber, in this example, replied '£5.36 to £5.40', indicating he would buy BP shares at the lower price or sell them at the higher. The gap provided the jobber's 'turn' or margin, in other words, his livelihood. With a share as well known as BP, the jobber would more probably have answered 'thirty-six to forty', correctly assuming that any dealer would have known that the price was in the area of £5.

The dealer would then visit other stalls, much as a cost-conscious shopper might seek the best price for a cauliflower, and obtains alternative quotes. Having settled on the most attractive, and still without disclosing whether he was a buyer or a seller, the dealer then reapproached one of the jobbers, reminded him of the quote he had made a few minutes earlier, and asked if there was a possibility of 'anything closer'.

The jobber, sniffing the possibility of an imminent deal, would try to guess whether his client was a buyer or seller, and would then ask: 'Are you many?'. 'Only 500', said the broker, in the knowledge that small packages were usually attractive to jobbers, who, at the end of the trading account, have to balance up buyers with sellers. 'I'll make you thirty-six to thirty-nine and a half,' the jobber replied. In turn the broker said: 'I'll sell you 500 at thirty-six,' and a 'bargain' is struck. This is recorded on a slip of paper in the notebook of each party.

Under Stock Exchange etiquette, the broker was obliged to deal at the time of the quote, he could not have returned ten minutes later, having haggled elsewhere. Had he decided not to deal, the jobber would have said formally: 'I'm off,' indicating that the quote was no longer valid.

The End of an Era

To some the well-established system of buying and selling shares through jobbers via brokers seemed eternal. After all, as we have seen, it offered the benefit of a truly constant market. Buyers and their brokers did not have to wait hours or even days before finding someone willing to sell them shares. The cut-and-thrust nature of jobbing was there to make sure that fair, competitive prices were always available, while the rule requiring deals to pass through jobbers prevented brokers from selling stock to customers at artificially high prices.

But market forces and modern technology were threatening this system even before its abolition in October 1986.

Such had been the impact of taxation and inflation on individual savings in the 1960s and 1970s that the private investor was all but lost to the market, leaving the power, and the money, with the pensions and savings funds. These institutional investors did not see the point of paying fixed broking commissions, which could run into the tens of thousands of pounds, for a simple deal that could as well be conducted by telephone. They did not see the need for the brokers' research, since they had their own staff of fund managers and analysts. And as, increasingly, they wanted to buy large parcels of stock, they, or rather their brokers, found the jobbers hard-pressed to find it from their own books and even less willing to take a big risk with the price.

So the institutions started dealing among themselves. They were also helped by a computerized system called Ariel, which was set up by the merchant banks so that fund managers could be kept in touch with transactions and prices as bargains were struck. Soon, knowing the price, fund managers were using Ariel to trade.

It was only a matter of time before what has been termed the dual-dealing system cracked. Stockbrokers began taking shares in firms of stockjobbers, and vice versa. The final push for change came when, as mentioned in Chapter I, the Government's Office of Fair Trading brought the legal action against the Stock Exchange charging that the practice of fixed commissions was unfair, and against the public interest. Without the prop of high commissions from trading between institutions, the single-capacity dealing system, as it was called, was doomed.

Almost as contentious an issue as ending the dual-dealing system was what should replace it. One had only to look at the other major stock exchanges around the world to discover that there were not many choices. One common system was the auction, where shares were traded in a not dissimilar method to cattle at a country market; the cattle go to the highest bidder, or, at least, to the one who can shout the loudest. In the case of share auctions a person with a parcel to sell would make the fact known and stand advertising his wares on the Exchange floor until he found an acceptable buyer, who might or might not pay the highest price. If the broker was tired on his feet, or suffering from laryngitis, he might be tempted to sell out cheap.

The Council of the Stock Exchange, in their perambulations around the world to discover a *modus operandi* that could be sold to their members, found much to their liking in the United States, through what is called the NASDAQ system. NASDAQ stands for National Association of Securities Dealers Automatic Quotation System, and it means what it says. Whenever a dealer makes a market – in other words provides a quote for the purchase or sale of a stock – he enters it into his terminal, which is on line to a national data base, to which all marketmakers subscribe. Securities dealers in over 6,000 offices have at their finger tips an exact, national, instantaneous wholesale price system, available in San Francisco, Chicago or Dallas at the same time as Wall Street. Indeed, it goes beyond that. There are over 8,500 quotation terminals outside the United States, most of them, about 5,000, in Europe.

Members of NASDAQ may act either as principals or agents. The principal, or market-maker, bears a close resemblance to a broker, except that instead of leaning against a bench in a crowded exchange, he is usually in an air-conditioned suite surrounded by monitors, banks of command telephones, and girls whose language leaves much to be desired. At any time during the day, he may enter against the name of a company a price at which he is prepared to buy its stock, and a price at which he will sell it. From time to time, he will update his quote, and he will follow news developments closely over the Reuter Money Line service. He trusts and hopes his price will be competitive with other market-makers in NASDAQ, and confidently waits for a telephone call from a broker thirsting to buy.

The NASDAQ system is of benefit also to anyone else in the investment business, from brokers in San Antonio to the man on the stockbroker counter at the local Sears Roebuck department store, and to those in London who want instant information about the American market. There is nothing to stop individual investors subscribing, and NASDAQ already has over 100,000 hooked up, including brokers who are members of the London Stock Exchange. Those who pay a small subscription have access to the system through a dumb terminal and a black and white monitor. By using a word code on the terminal keyboard, they can obtain on the screen a representative 'bid' and a representative 'ask' price on the stock; for example, if dealers or market-makers have quoted bids on a particular stock of 40, 40.25, 40.50, 40.75, and 41, the representative bid would be 40.5. If those with a terminal wish to buy or sell – or if their customer so wishes – all they have to do is to phone their broker and seek a real quote, asking that it should be close to the representative figure on the screen, and stipulating, if they wish, how far from the figure they are prepared to trade.

NASDAQ has a more sophisticated, and more expensive, service for professional traders. In this case, having obtained a representative quote, a user may then seek actual quotes from the firms making the market in the stock. This is what would happen if an individual using the basic service were to phone in. The screen would display all those offering a quote, together with their names and telephone numbers, ranked in order of best price. The final barter then takes place over the telephone, and the new quote is inputted on the screen, with the computer updating the representative or average price. It will not be long before such telephone contact becomes unnecessary, and the transaction can be completed by keyboarding the computer.

All deals in securities that are traded regularly and in large volume – a list of about 2,000 stocks – must be reported within 90 seconds of the trade taking place. There are safeguards built into the NASDAQ system to attempt to prevent malpractice, and to seek to provide the investor with the same security that he had under the London jobbing system. Dealers must have a net capital of $25,000, or $2,500 for each security in which they are registered, whichever happens to be the greater. Once registered in a stock, a NASDAQ dealer must be prepared to buy or sell at any time, in much the same way as a jobber has been obliged to stand behind his price. There must be at least two market-makers for each stock quoted.

A market-maker whose spread – the difference between his 'buy' and 'sell' quotation – is more than double that of the representative or average spread, will be warned by the computer that his spread is excessive. The computer warning also finds its way into the directories of the National Association of Security Dealers, which will almost certainly call for an explanation, and may take disciplinary action.

Another safety measure is a provision in the NASDAQ rules that when a member dealer buys on his own account and not on behalf of a client, he should do so at a price which is 'fair' in relation to the prices being made by the market-makers. The factors which should be taken into account by both members and disciplinary committees in determining the fairness of such deals are set out in the association's Rules of Fair Practice, and include the type of security and its availability in the market.

All members of NASDAQ must be members of the Securities Investor Protection Corporation, established by Congress in 1970; this means that those who buy and sell through the system have exactly the same protection as they would if they were dealing on the New York Stock Exchange. If an investor, or anyone else, feels he had been maltreated, or that there has been malpractice, the SIPC will contact the Association, which maintains a three-year computer file record of every price movement in a stock, and may trace the history of a stock second by second, identifying when changes took place, who initiated them, and what was the root cause. With such a complete audit trail, investigations are relatively easy to conduct.

NASDAQ, with 4,000 companies listed on its system, 5,000 brokerage firms as members, and an annual turnover of 16 billion shares, averaging a daily turnover of 64 million, is the third largest stock market in the world. It far exceeds London, and is only second to New York and Tokyo.

The Birth of SEAQ

For NASDAQ read SEAQ, which stands for Stock Exchange Automated Quotations System, meaning that share trading no longer involves paper on the floor of the Stock Exchange, but takes place electronically wherever an authorized dealer has access to a computer terminal and a telephone.

SEAQ replaced the old system on October 27 1986. Instead of jobbers manning their pitches on the floor of the

Exchange, a new breed known as market makers sit facing their screens and tapping into the SEAQ system the prices at which they are willing to buy and sell the shares of those companies in which they are authorized to make a market. Most market makers are at their desks at eight in the morning to review the papers rather like a punter studying the form. Once a bid and offer price have been entered, the market maker is obliged to trade at that price, although of course he can alter his figures at any time in response to market conditions – in other words after he has seen what the opposition is doing. The SEAQ system covers more than 3,500 securities, and is divided into three groups of stocks – alpha, beta, and gamma.

As the name implies alpha stocks are the most actively traded shares, and market makers who buy or sell must immediately enter the trade into the SEAQ system. From SEAQ the trade details are passed instantly to TOPIC, the Stock Exchange's electronic information service, which is available to traders, brokers and investors at varying levels of sophistication. Stock Exchange members authorized to trade get the complete picture – the range of quotes from all the market makers and the details of the last transaction in each stock. Other subscribers – investment institutions, private investors, journalists and basically anyone prepared to pay – get a trimmed down version which provides a single best quote for each SEAQ security held in the database, and, for alpha stocks, the number of trades in the previous five minutes and for the day as a whole.

So, to return to the example of the investor purchasing 500 shares in British Petroleum, how does the new system work? His broker or licenced financial intermediary SEAQ, he will call out the BP page from the system, and see an array of offers from more than a dozen market-makers, each of them identified by a code. One line will say 'HGVA 36–40 1 × 1'. This means that Hoare Govett, for example, are prepared to buy BP at £5.36 and to sell at £5.40, and that their figure applies for purchases or sales of 1,000 shares or less. Another line might say 'GRVA 36–41 1 × 2', indicating that Grieveson Grant will buy at the same price as Hoare Govett, but that they will only sell BP at £5.41, and then only in units of up to 2,000.

Another page on SEAQ will reveal that ten minutes earlier there had been a large transaction of BP shares at £5.38. Assuming he wants to trade, the broker calls the dealing desk of his own or another firm and asks to buy BP at £5.40. If the broker's firm is also listed as a market-maker in BP, the broker will try and keep the deal 'in-house' by persuading his own colleagues to match the Hoare Govett offer, which they may or may not be willing to do. When the bargain is struck, the market-maker enters it into the BP SEAQ page; other market-makers, noting the transaction, readjust their offers accordingly.

Deals in beta stocks are conducted in exactly the same way, except that not all trades are logged, and there are fewer market-makers, perhaps only two or three, who will usually be firms that have decided to specialize in a particular sector, such as electronics, or insurance. In the case of gamma stocks, only indicative quotes are provided, so that any broker anxious to consider a purchase has to call the market-maker and negotiate a price, often based on volume. Many of the market-makers in the gamma section may be regional brokers, who know companies in their area well and are better placed to hold the book than a large London conglomerate.

The new system removes completely the disadvantages once suffered by provincial stockbrokers. Not only may they act as market-makers in regional stocks, but they have the same instant access to pricing enjoyed by those whose offices are only yards away from the Stock Exchange, and will no longer be obliged to deal only as agents of a firm whose dealers patrol the Stock Exchange floor. The new system is also capable of accommodating many more members, who may live in a different time zone altogether, such as Hong Kong or Bahrein, although such firms would have the added burden of having to meet the laws in their own countries as well as the strict rules of the Stock Exchange. But it is probable that some offshore centres will accept the British regulations as their own, and therefore offer the prospect of substantial new markets for securities traded through SEAQ.

One danger seen in the new system is that, because there is no longer a strictly independent intermediary, the jobber, who lives or dies by judging the market price correctly, brokers can in theory sell to each other at prices which might bear little relation to the market, thereby feathering their own nests. Furthermore, if the market-maker has taken on a bad stock and made a loss on it, one of his dealers could attempt to unload it on an unsuspecting investor. If this happened on a small scale, there would be a few aggrieved investors who presumably would never deal with the firm again. If it happened on a large scale, there would be a major outcry. Such practices, of course, are strictly proscribed by the rules, and in the United States the powerful Securities and Exchange Commission, discussed in Chapter 9, maintains a close watch on share dealings.

Through SEAQ, the Stock Exchange is confident that such crooked practices will be detected and wiped out, and the Stock Exchange's own surveillance unit maintains a close watch on unusual pricing and share movements, monitored by a very powerful computer programme. Under the new Stock Exchange rules, where no market-maker is involved, reporting must be done by the broker executing a deal reporting by telephone or telex to the Exchange, where the trade will be entered into the SEAQ system for the purpose of surveillance. So even if the unwary client has not realized that he has been charged too much for a particular stock, there is a fair chance that the 26 inspectors at the Stock Exchange will have spotted that the price paid is out of line. If the client himself believes that he is the victim of a scam, all he has to do is to inform the Exchange of the exact time the deal was struck, which will be recorded on all future contract notes. The Exchange will replay the relevant SEAQ database (all tapes will be kept for five years) and will immediately be able to spot whether the price was a genuine error or the result of sharp practice. A tracer is also put on the deal, and any related transactions. It was this system that spotted unusual movements that led to the downfall of a leading executive of Morgan Grenfell in November 1986.

For the technically-minded, the SEAQ system operates on two dedicated mainframe computers, designed to respond to entries within one second, update information at a peak rate of 20 items per second, and handle up to 70,000 transactions an hour. This is more than twice the 1984 total market volume of trades. In the event of a computer crash, a major fire or bomb outrage at the Stock Exchange, all the records would be saved, for parallel computers operate in another part of London and, for double protection, in the United States. The entire capitalist system is not likely to fail because of a power cut!

Brokers and dealers get their information through an IBM-PC, or compatible equivalent, connected to the SEAQ system either by direct data line or, in the case of the smaller user or provincial broker, by a leased telephone line. Those who wish to use the system only occasionally may do so through an ordinary phone line, connecting their computer to the jack via a standard modem. Those on the move may use portable equipment, with an acoustic coupler.

For all this high-blown technology, SEAQ has not been without its problems; indeed the first few weeks of its trading life were a disaster. In the first few days after 'Big Bang' market makers discovered that it was taking half an hour or longer for changed prices entered into the system to appear on the information screens: the result was that most of them had no choice but to put the red light across their quotes, an indication that they were no longer prepared to trade. The alternative would have been to lose millions by trading at an out-of-date price.

But for those large financial conglomerates anxious to establish themselves as market makers in their new order, stopping trading was also unacceptable because no trades meant no income. With literally millions of pounds invested in new computer equipment and highly paid operatives, the new giants complained bitterly, releasing a tirade of criticism at what they believed to be the complacency of the Stock Exchange.

Certainly these criticizms seemed justified. First of all the Exchange said the complaints had been exaggerated by the media, when in fact the opposite was the case. Most City journalists, not being computer literate themselves, were slow to grasp the enormity of the problem. Then the Exchange blamed the failure of its computers on a widespread curiosity to see the new system at work, which led to it being overloaded. It was some time before the planners in Throgmorton Street came clean, and admitted that they should have increased the system's capacity by 100 per cent, not 50 per cent. Services were scaled down, particularly on TOPIC, which was proving totally inadequate for the key task of distributing new prices fast, and belated but intensive efforts were made to plug software and hardware gaps.

By early 1987 many of the teething problems had been, if not cured, alleviated, while both dealers and market makers alike showed considerable dexterity in coming to terms with the new system. Six months after 'Big Bang', it was hard to conceive that trading had been carried out any other way, and there was talk of closing down trading on the Stock Exchange floor altogether, and preserving it as a museum piece.

Handling the paperwork

The new system has cut down the paperwork, although recently that has already been much reduced as a result of the Stock Exchange introducing what is known as the Talisman system. Until then the striking of a deal between jobber and broker led to a paperchase of such proportions that stockbrokers had to employ over 5,000 settlement staff, and this, with office space and equipment, was costing in 1981 over £100m. a year. For although the broker and the jobber were bound by the Stock Exchange code of *Dictum Meum Pactum*, 'My Word is my Bond', an elaborate system was needed to ensure that shares purchased did end up in the deed-box of the buyer.

The details of all transactions recorded in the broker's dealing book were entered in ledgers, or computer programs, back at the office. The client was sent a contract note and a share registration form, which he had to return, together with an account. In London there were 22 accounting periods during the year, and statements were normally sent out after each one. Anyone who bought and sold their shares during an accounting period – a short-term speculator, for instance – would not have to pay for them.

The jobber's dealing record was also committed to ledgers back in his office, and it was here that the paper chain began. If he had bought shares in the market, say 1,000 ICI, he would expect to be able to find someone to take them over before the end of the account period, relieving him of the necessity to chase up the scrip. In the example where he sold 500 BP shares, things might have been more difficult. Within the accounting period he would expect to come across a seller of BP shares, hopefully prepared to sell at less than he had sold the earlier lot for, to enable him to cover his position and to make a profit.

But where he was a seller of shares, he faced the task of producing the scrip; in other words, to ensure that the share certificates were passed to the broker acting for the purchaser. With small parcles this was relatively easy, but where large trades occur, he might incur some difficulty. In any event it was unlikely that he would be able to match the sale exactly, so to obtain the scrip for any one parcel sold, he might have to go to several sellers for shares, thereby necessitating several contract notes to complete the transaction.

Back in the broker's office, clerks had to enter details of all these transactions into several other ledgers. There was the client ledger, dealing with each customer's transactions, which formed the basis of client billing. There was a list book, classified under the names of shares, to keep track of all trades. Each day clerks from broking houses would meet in the settlement room at the Stock Exchange to check the bargains reported by their dealers. Sometimes, in the mêlée of a busy day, errors occurred. Where the error was not the obvious fault of any one party, losses would be divided.

Once clients buying shares had returned their registration documents and settled their accounts, the broker had to make sure the relevant share certificates were provided to them. Share certificates were delivered by the selling brokers to the Central Stock Payment Office of the Stock Exchange, sorted into correct destinations, and collected by messengers of the buying brokers. For the reason explained earlier, in many cases there was more than one certificate, often from more than one individual. In the case of someone buying 1,000 ICI shares, for example, the certificates would come in odd lots, perhaps from different parts of the country. Details of the names and addresses of the former owners of the certificates would have to be recorded in yet another ledger, before the certificates were scrutinized by clerks for authenticity, and then sent off, together with the transfer authority, to the share registry of the company concerned. Very few listed companies, whether large or small, maintain their own share registry, preferring to pay for the services of specialist registrars, often operated by bank departments scattered around the country. Lloyds Bank's Registry department at Goring-on-Sea is one such registrar, and has become one of the largest employers in West Sussex; during the height of the British Telecom flotation it was handling more than one million pieces of mail a day. The system had barely changed for two centuries, and by 1980 it had become costly and grindingly slow. With up to half a million tickets and transfer forms passing round the market at the end of each account period, it was often many weeks before the purchaser of shares received the evidence of his purchase, by which time he might well have sold them again. It was costing registrars £75m. a year to maintain the share registers for just 9,000 securities.

The Talisman system

The definition of the Talisman system given in the Stock Exchange brochure speaks for itself. 'Talisman, tal'is-man, or-iz-n. Transfer Accounting Lodgement for Investors, Stock Management for jobbers: Gr. payment, certificate, later completion; or an object indued with magical powers through which extraordinary results are achieved' Given the cumbersome nature of the old system, it is not surprising that the Stock Exchange is lyrical about Talisman; anything which can cut out such a complicated paperchase would be credited with magical powers. Yet the theory behind Talisman is very simple.

Under Talisman the title of each share changing hands is transferred from its registered owner to Sepon Ltd, which is a Stock Exchange nominee company formed to hold shares in trust on behalf of the underlying new owner, whose interests are at all times fully protected. Sepon Ltd then transfers the shares on to the buying client.

It works like this. When the selling broker receives the share certificate and the returned signed transfer form from his client, he deposits them at the nearest Talisman centre, either in London or at one of eight other centres located in major British cities. At the Talisman centre the documents are checked for accuracy, and the transfer information – the names and addresses of the sellers and the contract price –

entered into the central computer system. This is based in the Stock Exchange building in London on two computers, with the entire system being periodically operated at another site in Britain.

The documents are then passed from the Talisman centre to the company's registrar for registration out of the client's name and into that of Sepon Ltd, although control of the stock remains with the selling client until payment is made and delivery effected. When that happens ownership is transferred within the Talisman computer to the buying jobber's – or market-maker's – account. Individual items of stock lose their identity, and simply become a pool of shares with which to satisfy buyers. The buying broker simply calls up Talisman and the purchase information is entered into the computer, which generates bought transfers, authorizing the removal of shares from the Sepon account into the name of the buying client. These bought transfers are sent on to the registrar, who transfers registration out of Sepon, and posts off a new share certificate to the purchaser.

The Talisman system also generates accounts for over 200 member firms of the Stock Exchange located in 65 cities and towns. By belonging to the network, each firm has only to write (or bank) one cheque in each accounting period. The system acts as a clearing-house between all the member firms, apportioning debits and credits, and providing them with a detailed statement, which they use to check their own records. Talisman also calculates payments due to the Inland Revenue for stamp duty, pays them regularly in bulk, and debits brokers' accounts.

The system has important benefits for investors, especially. over matters such as dividends, bonus issues and rights issues, which often become payable either just before or immediately after a sale of shares. The legal date for entitlement to dividends and such issues is the date of registration, and because Talisman has speeded up the registration process, annoying disputes can be avoided. Dividends received by Sepon Ltd are passed immediately to the entitled party.

Talisman is also used to settle international trades, providing benefits to those who deal through members or affiliates of the Stock Exchange. South African registered securities may be settled through the system; indeed for those investing in South African stocks it provides by far the swiftest way of doing so, and well before the end of the decade similar links will have been created with the other major share trading centres.

The new dealing rooms

The effect of SEAQ, Talisman, and other computerized systems which speed and automate share dealing and registration has been to change the look of stockbrokers' offices. Most broker's offices now include two vast open-plan areas – the dealing room, and the processing room, both of them carpeted, comfortable and sound-proofed.

Dealers sit at consoles with screens, which bring them instant price information – from SEAQ on the Stock Exchange's Topic, Reuters international network, and Telerate and Quotron, which are American systems. They can split the screen four ways if they wish, or switch instantly from one to another. Some deals are carried out by telephone, using numbers dialled directly by computer, and others are entered directly into terminals. A microphone record and time-code on tape deals as they are carried out. In the other room all the details will immediately be entered in the brokers' own computer, which will send them on at once to the computers of the self-regulatory agency.

Typical of today's dealing rooms is that of Barclays De Zoete Wedd, sited in a large block overlooking the Thames just below London Bridge. It is the size of a large sports centre, laid out with rows of desks logically organized. At one end of the floor are the analysts, their desks piled high with paper and reports, the level of conversation earnest, even muted. Adjoining them are the equity salesmen, men and women who used to like to call themselves brokers. They sit at terminals, and spend most of the time on the phone to institutions or private clients, discussing the prospect of buying or selling shares. If a client wants to know the price of any given share they can tell him instantly, by calling it up on the SEAQ screen, and if a more detailed assessment of long term prospects is called for they may ask one of the analysts to pick up the call. When a client is ready to buy or sell they normally shout the order to the market makers at the next bank of desks. When a BZW salesmen places an order through a BZW market maker the client must be offered the best price available on the SEAQ screen; if colleagues at the next desk are unable or unwilling to match the best price, then the deal must be done through the rival market maker, an important new rule to ensure that investors are not put at a disadvantage as a result of the end of the dual capacity jobbing system.

The Americans Ride In

While the Council of the Stock Exchange was considering which system it would introduce, those who were going to operate it began to form new alliances that have changed the face of British stockbroking. Throgmorton Street is now dominated by foreigners, for only a minority of the major firms are left under British ownership, the only financial centre in the world where this is so.

Famous old London firms gratefully accepted the offers of cash up front and capital injections. Many found their saviours across the Atlantic. Vickers da Costa and Scrimgeour Gee came under the wing of Citicorp, America's largest bank. Laurie Milbank and Simon and Coates embraced the Chase Manhattan Bank, while Savory Milln joined up with Dow Scandia. Panmore Gordon found a place in the sun with the Florida-based NCNB Corporation.

Although the American banks were the most aggressive, other foreign banks also moved in with a vengeance. The Australians, through their ownership of Grindlay's Bank, bought Capel-Cure Myers, the Hongkong and Shanghai Banking Group swallowed up James Capel and Co., Crédit Suisse moved to control Buckmaster and Moore, and the forthright (and very good) economic commentator, Dr Paul Neild of Phillips and Drew, found he was working for the notoriously reticent Union Bank of Switzerland. Even the chairman of the Stock Exchange's firm, Quilter Goodison, linked up with the Swedish insurance group, Skandia, which gained a 30 per cent stake.

The British merchant banks also wanted a slice of the action. Kleinwort Benson took over Grieveson Grant, Samuel Montague joined W. Greenwell and Co., Morgan Grenfell took over Pinchin Denny and Pember and Boyle, Baring Brothers linked with Henderson Crosthwaite, and Hill Samuel with Wood Mackenzie.

Some, like Lloyds Bank chose not to form mergers. In explaining their reasons, Lloyds executives struck a chord with many in the market who fear that too much money has been paid by too many people to acquire very little. After all, when you buy a stockbroker, you are really only buying people who can, and do, leave for other, greener pastures, usually the competition. 'We did not think the prices made sense,' was the view of Lloyds Merchant Bank managing director, Piers Brooke. 'We felt the cultural problems would further compound the problem of generating the returns we were looking for.'

Sir John Nott, chairman of Lazard Brothers, and one of those concerned about conflict of interest and fraud problems in the new City, concurs. 'The prices which have been paid for brokers and jobbers are quite beyond their likely earning power'. Some American bankers agree. 'They are ridiculous,' says Samuel Armacost, president of the Bank of America. 'The economics of it fail me. I just don't see how the people who bought some of those things for some of those prices can look their shareholders in the eye. I twice threw guys out of my office who came in with proposals.'

Even Merrill Lynch, the world's largest stockbroker, has been adopting a cautious approach, deciding against buying a large Stock Exchange firm, but instead hiring one of the City's most prominent personalities, Stanislas Yassukovich from the European Banking Corporation, who immediately bewailed the fact that working for the Americans would mean giving up polo and his five polo ponies. Yassukovich, who became deputy chairman of the Stock Exchange was, doubtful whether Big Bang would generate more business, but concurred with his chairman Bill Schreyer that Merrill Lynch was well-positioned in terms of capital, people and talent. 'The strong will survive' and 'The old school tie connection will go out of the window.'

A senior executive with Barclays De Zoete Wedd agrees with the City consensus that profits will 'take years to arrive'. 'For some they will never come, for they will go bust first. But we have to do this, and we have to be strong enough to last the pace.' David Scholey, chairman of S. G. Warburg and Co., whose link-up with Rowe and Pitman, Mullens & Co., and Ackroyd and Smithers, had formed the Mercury International Group, also argues that his organization had no choice once it had evaluated the alternative of limiting itself to carving out a specialist niche rather than competing in the major league:

> Going for the niche solution would have meant telling our clients that we could only offer selected financial advice or that we might be able to offer advice but would not be directly involved in its implementation. Inevitably we would gradually lose our knowledge of the whole range of our clients' financial activities because we would only be seeking to be involved in part of them. We would also have lost the feel for markets. Thus the question of how we should plan our future admitted of only one answer for us.

The £500m. or so committed to new City alliances is, of course, not the only cost. Partners in broking firms bought out for £20m. apiece – or more – can retire, or continue to work in comfort. But dealers, analysts, and market-makers all want their share of the action, and are demanding, and getting, enormous salaries. Top gilts dealers in late 1985 were earning on average £250,000 – rather above the average pay for the Chief executive of a large British public company – while top Eurobond dealers can demand about £300,000. Senior executives in the new conglomerates will be looking for between £300,000 and £500,000, and a senior analyst will be on £100,000, plus bonuses, which in the case of at least one broker in 1985 amounted to 165 per cent.

The highest salaries were gathered by those prepared to move jobs, some shifting in packs. Not long after Barclays acquired Wedd Durlacher Mordaunt, the gilts market-maker, eight senior dealers defected to Kleinwort Benson, much to the irritation of Barclays De Zoete Wedd, which threatened to sue. Another seven Wedd Durlacher people promptly defected to Savory Milln. Barclays retaliated by poaching Sir Martin Jacomb, vice-chairman of Kleinwort, to head its investment banking side. The entire breweries research team of Fielding Newsom-Smith went to BZW, after receiving an advance payment, better known as a golden hallo or golden handcuff, as well as huge salaries. One 21-year-old woman gilts dealer who moved from a British company to an American one doubled her salary to $50,000, though still remaining a relatively junior member of the team. Some people feel that the imbalance caused by jobhoppers netting enormous salaries and perks while others co-exist on much lower pay will cause lasting damage. A leading salaries' consultant told me:

> The problem is particularly difficult for the clearing banks, for they have been used to graded pay structures. Now you are going to find a bank analyst or economist sitting next door to a broker's economist, and the brokers' man will be earning twice as much. It will not be good for morale, but the banks will not want the new higher salaries to spread through their whole system. The real trouble will come when the bear market arrives, and business turns down. There will then be a really rather substantial blood-bath. A lot of people will be sacked.

My consultant friend itemized the problems: a blending problem with different styles of management between brokers and bankers, the tendency for whole teams to move, the pressure for equal pay with the US in US-owned firms, and the fact that in the new conglomerates 'many at the top are good dealers but pretty hopeless managers'.

> When they have come to hire new people they approach it as they approach a deal, asking themselves 'can I get him and how much will it cost?' The trouble is they never ask themselves whether the new people will fit in.

The Bank of England has already taken the new conglomerates to task for the high salaries they are paying, but to no avail. It is difficult to see what the Bank can do about it, except to express its disapproval in comments like the following from the Deputy Governor:

> Both the fact that abnormally high salaries are being offered to key groups of staff and the publicity it has attracted are unwelcome: the more so, because the insecurity which one might expect to accompany such salary levels does not yet seem to be much in evidence. More thought, I suggest, needs to be given to what it is that these salaries are being paid for, and whether they are justified.

Whether justified or not, the higher salaries will undoubtedly lead to cut-throat competition and, as Merrill Lynch's chairman says, the welcome end of the old-boy network in the Square Mile. The City, under American influence, will also go in for more razmatazz. That trend, to some extent, is already under way. Market analysts are now being given VIP treatment by major corporations, with trips to favoured European watering holes now a common event. It presumably will be only a matter of time before London emulates some of the fun and games in New York, where, it seems, there is almost no limit to the lengths to which a stockbroker will go to keep his clients happy. One such figure, Alecko Papamarkou, who coined the phrase 'Nouveau is better than no Riche at all', endeared himself to gossip columnists when he transported 100 clients on a cruise down the Nile. Papamarkou, who numbers sheikhs and film stars among his clients, is an individualist, without much time for the bigger Wall Street firms, which he dubs 'pathetic'. 'They are very bureaucratic', he says, adding that he regrets 'all that time wasted fighting for commissions, or fighting to keep from being cheated by your higher-ups, who are neither financiers nor good administrators'.

Selling Gilts

A crucial aspect of the new Stock Exchange's work is the gilts market – the mechanism by which the British Government funds its public sector borrowing requirement.

The PSBR – as it is known in Whitehall and in the media – is the gap between the total amount of Government spending – on such essentials as defence, health, education, welfare and the whole apparatus of Whitehall – and the total amount it receives from the British taxpayer.

Guided by the Treasury officials, the Bank of England, and the Government broker – a leading City firm, Mullens and Co. has held this office for over a century – the Chancellor of the Exchequer taps the Stock Market when it seems most propitious to do so – if possible, when interest rates are falling and there are no other huge calls on funds available. Hence the frequent use of the phrase 'tap-stock'.

Like other fixed-interest securities, such as bonds issued

by large corporations and local authorities, the prices of gilt-edged securities are sensitive to alterations in spot and anticipated interest rates, and move up and down. The London gilt market is a huge one, worth over £275bn., second only to those of Japan and the United States, and gilts are issued on amounts of from £1m. to £2.5m. for periods of one to 35 years.

Until 1986 this market had been the preserve of a privileged few gilts jobbers, with two firms, Ackroyd and Smithers and Wedd Durlacher Mordaunt, controlling 85 per cent of the dealing. Commissions were modest, for jobbers had to earn their keep by anticipating changes in interest rates and positioning prices accordingly, before selling both newly issued gilts and traded stock on to brokers, who in turn marketed them to investors, deducting their commission on the way. Again there was a limited number of brokers dominating the market – Mullens and Co., W. Greenwell and Co., Grieveson Grant, Hoare Govett and Phillips and Drew. But, in October 1986, the Bank of England opened up to 29 firms in a free-for-all.

The 29 received Bank of England approval to act as market-makers under its own strict supervision, rather than that of the Stock Exchange. Each was given a borrowing facility at the Bank of England and access to a new electronic gilts clearing-house. Those working as market-makers may belong or be affiliated to a general financial house, but themselves must trade only in sterling debt securities and related instruments, such as gilt-edged futures and traded options (which we shall deal with in the next section).

The new gilts market is largely telephone-based. Dealers sit at a trading desk in their office, and salesmen located within earshot shout orders for them to negotiate by phone with other market-makers. Prices are based on market-makers' judgements.

Almost everyone in the City accepts that not all gilts market makers will survive, and that some will certainly pull out licking their wounds after incurring heavy losses. It is also feared that the costs of dealing are going to rise, not least because of the salaries being paid and the carving up of the market among a greater number than under the old system. The Bank of England, which issued the licences, does not accept this at all, but there is no doubt truth in the suggestion that the authorities preferred the market to sort out the winners and losers.

Options and Futures

'If you are very good at market triming, you can make out like a bandit', said Donald Mesler of Chicago, author of *Stock Market Options*.

Options

For those prepared to risk a little money on speculation, options offer an attractive prospect. Many people have been heard to say: 'I would like to be able to buy shares in BP, ICI, or Hanson Trust, but their prices are so high I could not possibly afford them.' Leaving aside the loose logic of that statement – for an individual can always buy 50 or even 25 shares if he wishes – it is true that the chances of a major capital gain on one of the large and better known shares are slim.

That is, unless the investor wishes to try options. For example, let us say that on 19 December an individual thinks that Marks and Spencer is going to achieve record Christmas sales and that the margins will be such as to generate handsome profits for the company in the current financial year. He fancies chancing about £1,000 on his belief that the shares will rise. But at 175p. each – the price on 19 December 1985 – £1,000 will buy him only about 570 shares. If, in the months ahead, the share price rises to 190p. – a level it had achieved earlier in 1985 – our friend will have made a capital gain of £85.50, less two lots of brokerage charges plus Value Added Tax. On options he would have done much better. His £1,000 would have bought him almost 7,700 3-month call options at a cost of 13p. each – the premium quoted on 19 December. This gives him the right to buy those 7,700 shares at any time in the next three months, at the 19 December price of 175p. When the shares rise to 190p., therefore, he will have made a capital gain of £1,155 – in other words a return in excess of 110 per cent on his original investment. He will not even have to find the money to pay for them, provided he buys and sells within the same Stock Exchange accounting period. However, should the shares fall over the three-month period by 15p. each, he will either have to find the full cost of 7,700 shares – in this example it would be about £13,500 – or forfeit the option to buy, which means that his £1,000 outlay has been lost.

If the stock is one in which the Stock Exchange runs a traded options market, then the investor has another possibility open to him, and that is to sell the option to another investor. The price of a traded option is decided by two factors: the underlying price of the share itself, and the market's expectations as to which way it will move in the weeks or months ahead. Obviously those operating in the traded options market expect to make a profit, so there is a premium to be paid for selling the unexpired portion of an option rather than sitting it out. But where an investor playing fears he has made a major misjudgement he can, to some extent, cover a big position by using the traded options market.

Another form of option is the 'put' option, which is the opposite of a 'call' option. A put option is taken out in anticipation of a fall in the value of the relevant share, and gives the owner the option to sell a quantity of shares at a given price.

It would be fair to say that so far in Britain the concept of investing in options has not caught on among general investors, although it plays a major part in the lives of the professionals. In the United States, where attidues are rather different, options are booming. The Chicago Board Options Exchange is the second largest securities market in the United States, behind only the New York Exchange. The US regulatory authorities are also strong supporters of options trading, with the Securities and Exchange Commission arguing that it significantly enhances liquidity. But if you imagine that by buying options you are sure to win a fortune, be warned by the following remark from Stephen Figlewski, the Associate Professor of Finance at New York University:

> Small investors lose because they believe their information is better than it really is. They take positions that aren't any better

than their beliefs, and their beliefs aren't any better than throwing darts.

Futures

If trading in options sounds a little like a casino, it is dull by comparison with the activities on the futures markets. There are futures in everything – commodities like cocoa, coffee, wheat, lead, zinc and gold; meats like cattle and pork; currencies like the dollar, the yen, the German Mark, and the pound; and of course, shares.

Buying futures is speculation, and some people make and lose millions by doing it. It requires knowledge of changing circumstances, as well as intuition as to the way events will turn out. If you think that there will be a severe frost in Brazil – or are prepared to bet that this will be so – you may buy 6-month coffee futures, in the belief that by the time your coffee is delivered at the end of the period, it will be worth a lot more. Of course, there is no need for you to take delivery of the coffee at all; if the frost comes, the price of your futures contract will rise sharply, and you may sell out.

There is, of course, good reason for buying futures other than speculation. If you are a coffee wholesaler and you fear a cold snap in Brazil, you will buy futures to protect yourself, regarding the extra cost of the contract as an insurance premium. The same is true of the manufacturing industry. If you have ordered an expensive set of machine tools from Germany, due to be delivered in six months' time, you will not want to pay for them until delivery. But supposing the pound falls against the Mark in the meantime? You cover yourself by buying the required amount of Deutschemark futures. This process is called 'hedging'.

There are futures markets in all the major financial centres, while Chicago has assumed pre-eminence in the trading of commodities. London was slow to see the potential of futures markets, but in September 1982, members of the Stock Exchange joined forces with banks and commodities brokers to establish LIFFE – the London International Financial Futures Exchange – in the Royal Exchange building adjacent to the Bank of England and close to the site of the famous old coffee houses. LIFFE futures and options contracts have the great advantage of being 'exchange traded', and so are claimed to be free of credit risk, while their prices are displayed worldwide. When LIFFE was opened it was hailed as an institution that could maintain London's place at the heart of the world's financial system and divert business from the United States, denting Chicago's supremacy. By early 1987, LIFFE was putting through 30,000 contracts a day, with most of the action concentrated in the Eurodollar, sterling, gilt-edged contracts.

The biggest growth in turnover is likely to be in the gilts and interest-rate contracts, for the increase in the number of gilt-edged market-makers to 29 in 1986 will place a premium on hedging contracts. For instance, a fund manager may know that in three months he will receive cash for investment in gilts, and he has picked long gilts – those maturing in 15 years' time. Rather than waiting to see what the interest rate will be at that time, he can lock into today's rate by buying LIFFE's long gilts futures contracts for delivery in three months' time. If gilt yields then decline, the investor will have to pay a higher price, but the price of the Long Gilts futures contracts will have risen, and the fund manager's profits will reduce the effective cost of buying the stock.

The FT-SE 100 futures contract is priced by taking one-tenth of the value of the FT-SE 100 Share Index published throughout each business day. It may be used by an investment manager concerned that the market will rise before he can place funds becoming available to him.

4 The Share Buyers

'Have I made thee more profit than other princes can?' – Prospero in The Tempest, Act I, Scene II.

Indirectly most of Britain's share buyers are you and me, but despite the stimulus provided by privatization individuals are not active traders; only about one in four of us owns any shares of our own. That said, there is hardly a family in the land which has not a vested interest in the success of equities and the growth of Stock Markets, both in the United Kingdom and elsewhere.

The majority owns shares through institutional investors: the pension funds, life assurance companies, unit trusts and investments trusts, which together employ over 7,000 people to manage their money. Their clout in the market through the size of their portfolios not only gives them enormous power in the operations of major companies but has also sparked off the mushroom growth of two stockmarket related industries: fund management and investment and financial public relations.

In 1985 the Bank of England undertook a study of investment management in Britain, and discovered that more than £100bn. was under management for United Kingdom residents, plus a further £50bn. of non-residents' funds. About half the funds were in equities, and one quarter of the money was invested abroad. The Bank rightly sees this as only the start. The 1974 Employee Retirement Income Security Act in the United States placed a requirement on pension fund managers to diversify in order to reduce the risk of losses. By the end of 1984, around £18bn. of US pension fund assets had been diversified into foreign assets, and this is likely to continue apace as the dollar weakens. Similar opportunities are available for British fund managers to manage pension fund assets from Canada, Japan and Australia, all of whom have recently relaxed their rules.

Pension Funds

Although often referred to with some animosity by socialist politicians as 'gnomes' and money manipulators, too powerful for their own and the country's good, Britain's institutional investors vary widely in their objectives. Pension funds – by far the most important, with well over £60bn. in assets – invest the contributions of employees and their employers with the objective of maximum gain, so that the obligations of their various schemes may be fully and easily met. They are not above a bit of speculation, but generally their funds are directed towards meeting the pledges made to employees without necessitating an increase in employers' contributions. The better a pension fund is managed, the lower the employer's cost. So most pension funds, including those run exclusively for the benefit of trade union members, allocate their investments across a broad spectrum, preferring a diversified portfolio, as the jargon puts it, to excessive concentration in one or two stocks, or venturing into risky projects. Almost all pension funds have, in recent years, also diversified their portfolios to include investments in the United States, Western Europe, and the Far East and Pacific Basin. When the pound was strong, and sterling a petro-currency, it made sense to buy shares in blue-chip, high-growth overseas enterprises, such as IBM in the United States, or Elders-IXL in Australia. As sterling slipped back, those holding large volumes of stock in strong currencies made huge capital gains from dollar holdings.

Life Assurance Companies

Then there are life assurance companies, whose principal concern is to ensure that the premium incomes received are invested adequately to meet the eventual pay-out upon death or the end of a term. It is necessary for these huge investors to match their known obligations, calculated through actuarial tables, with investments maturing at the same time. For this reason assurance companies invest heavily in long-dated gilt-edged securities or bonds.

Some governments insist that institutions like life assurance companies and pension funds, which are often the recipients of generous tax treatment, allocate a substantial proportion of their investments to gilt-edged securities or semi-government bonds. There is, however, a trend away from such rules. Australia, for instance, abolished what was known as the 20/30 rule whereby for every $30 invested elsewhere, $20 had to be invested in government bonds. Japan, whose pension funds have colossal clout, has gradually been easing the restrictions which made it difficult for large sums of money to be invested elsewhere than in Japanese industry.

The absence of regulation does not stop critics of capitalism objecting strongly to privileged institutional investors failing, in their view, to use their funds in the national interest. Present Labour Party policy in Britain is that pension funds should be obliged to invest much of their money in British industry. The counter-argument, of course, is that it is the duty of pension funds and life assurance companies to do the best they can for those whose money they hold in trust – future pensioners and policy-holders – and therefore their fund managers should be unfettered by nationalistic controls.

Both arguments have been well aired, and in the second half of the 1970s a Committee of Inquiry headed by the former Prime Minister, Harold Wilson, investigated the matter thoroughly, while also focusing specifically on the charge that lack of controls had denied British industry or would-be entrepreneurs adequate capital. In its report, published in June 1980, the Committee resoundingly rejected the charges, and to this day no solid evidence has been produced that worthwhile ventures are denied funds. If anything, the margin of error has been the other way: the City and institutional investors have been only too willing to bail out lame ducks that should have been allowed to pass into liquidation or more competent hands.

Unit Trusts

The other set of powerful institutional investors are unit trusts, investment trusts, and managed funds, which together manage about £30bn. of our savings. Unit trusts provide ways in which small and medium-sized investors can take an interest in equity markets, both in Britain and overseas, without having to take the risk of buying shares in individual companies.

There are over 750 unit trust funds in Britain alone, managed by 130 separate London groups. Some of the groups are very large; the Save and Prosper Group, for instance, had 700 people on its books in 1985. As a glance through the advertisements in the Saturday papers show, there is a unit trust for everybody: trusts that offer the prospect of capital gain, and those that offer income; trusts that invest in blue-chip stocks, and those that specialize in high-risk, or 'recovery', stocks. Almost all unit trust management companies, many of them owned by banks, merchant banks, or insurance companies, have specialist country funds. The most popular are those with portfolios in Western Europe, the United States, Japan and Australia, and the more stable countries of South East Asia – in other words stable economies which are part of the Organization for Economic Cooperation and Development club. There are, as far as I know, no unit trusts offering units in Chile, Zimbabwe, or the Soviet bloc, although, oddly enough, the Hungarian Government runs its own Luxembourg-based unit trust investing in equities in the Western world.

A good idea of the range available can be seen by looking at the funds managed by just one average group, Henderson Administration. In Britain it has five funds: Capital Growth, Income and Assets, Recovery, one called Special Situations which looks at major opportunities in the market place, and Financial, which has a portfolio of shares in banks and other financial institutions. It also has eight high income trusts, one of them specializing in smaller companies, another limited to UK government gilt-edged securities. On a global scale, Henderson has six funds, one of them limited to gold stocks, another to oil and natural resources, another to technology stocks, and another specializing in health stocks. Its ten overseas country funds are self-explanatory: Australian, European, European Small Companies, Japan Trust, Japan Social Situations, Pacific Small Companies, Singapore and Malaysia, North America, American Smaller Companies, and American Recovery. Finally there are seven 'exempt' funds designed specifically for the offshore investor – usually expatriates, such as an oilman working in Dubai, or an executive on a foreign posting.

Most unit trust managers also offer life or pension-linked funds, which allow the investor substantial tax advantages, in that the cost of units is permitted as a tax deduction so long as the investor does not sell the units or receive any dividends until retirement age. Just before Budget day, when there is almost annual press speculation that this juicy perk is to be removed, the financial pages of the major newspapers are thick with advertisements for pension-linked unit trusts.

Another form of unit trust investment which has become popular because of its tax efficiency is the umbrella fund, which allows investors to switch units between funds, without being liable for capital gains tax on any profit on the deal. This allows both fund managers and private investors to operate efficiently in the widely fluctuating foreign exchange markets; anyone moving in and out of American dollar equities at the right time during 1984 and 1985, for instance, would have enjoyed a substantial capital gain.

Unit trust investment is now more popular than building societies, with funds deposited rising by 50 per cent in value in 1986, the year of 'Big Bang'. There were, at the end of 1986, 3.34 million people holding units.

Although, in common with equities, unit trusts performed badly in the mid-1970s, they have produced adequate returns ever since. Indeed, except for those with homes in the south-east of England, they have offered a better return than real estate. Someone with a house in Liverpool, say, would have done better to have sold his house upon retirement five years ago, invested the fund in unit trusts, and rented a villa in the Algarve or Majorca.

Unit trusts have also, as the table shows, performed much better than building society share accounts, a traditional haven for the savings of the masses. This is especially significant for savers over a long period, who do not need to withdraw sums at short notice.

£1,000 invested over 5, 10 and 15 years

Fund	*5 yrs*	*10 yrs*	*15 yrs*
Japanese funds	3,302	4,258	10,659
North American	2,666	3,250	4,767
British funds	2,437	5,429	6,926
Building Society	1,485	2,142	2,883

On the other hand, over a short period, investment in unit trusts can lose money. A *Times* analysis of unit trust performance in 1985 found that 201 of 716 funds analysed were worth less at the end of the year than at the beginning; had savers put their money in building societies instead, only 288 of the funds would have produced a better return. Lloyds Bank customers would have been better leaving their money on deposit throughout 1985 than investing in any of the bank's unit trusts, with five of the nine trusts failing to break even.

This does not mean that it is more sensible to invest in a building society or bank – unless, of course, you are saving for a home, and need a mortgage. What it does mean is that you must pick your unit trust carefully. The same *Times*' survey pointed out that seven out of the nine unit trusts operated by Touche Remnant did better than building society investments; one of them performed outstandingly well, returning £49 for every £100 invested, and only one failed to break even.

One of the problems with unit trusts, from an investor's point of view, is that it costs rather too much to buy them. There is usually an up-front charge of 5 per cent, plus the burden of VAT, so that quite often it may be some time before the buyer can see any improvement in his portfolio. The spread between the bid and the offer price is also often large – 6 per cent or more, with some as high as 14 per cent – so your units will have to rise appreciably before you can sell them at profit. And the more you switch the more it costs, which may help the intermediary or discretionary portfolio adviser, but is no use to the investor at all.

There are also widespread differences in the performances of the various funds, a fact which seems to escape much public notice despite the fact that there is at least one major magazine dedicated to publishing comparisons, while those who can claim a good record shout it from the rooftops. The September 1985 issue of *Money Management* showed that over the previous 12 months FS Balanced Growth had been the best performing unit trust; £1,000 invested there would have more than doubled to £2,021 in the year. On the other hand, 1,000 invested in Henderson's Malaysia and Singapore Fund had fallen to only £662. The picture was just as interesting over a three-year span. An investment of £1,000 in GT's European Fund would have grown substantially to £2,816, while the same amount invested in Britannia's Hong Kong Performance Trust would have lost £26.

Of course these tables are about as useful as a league table in professional football. Just because you are top one month, does not mean that you will stay there. Many who bought Britannia Gold and General Trust when it became top performer in 1983 with 93.4 per cent growth did not anticipate that only one year later it would drop to the bottom of the table, losing investors £24 for every £1,000 invested. Even so there are definitely above-average and below-average performers, so why support a loser? It is interesting to look at the performance of unit trusts run by trading banks as well as those whose advertisements proliferate in the Sunday newspapers. By and large they are indifferent performers.

Investment Trusts

Often confused with unit trusts, but different in concept, are investment trusts. Like unit trusts, investment trusts allow the smaller private investor to benefit from having a stake in a large portfolio of widely spread shares, both by sector and by region. But there the similarity ends. Investment trusts are public companies like any other public company, and their shares are traded on the Stock Exchange; instead of making motor cars, running hotels, or operating department stores, an investment trust company exists purely and simply to buy and sell shares in other companies, both for short-term speculative gain and long-term capital growth. Those who manage investment trusts, full-time executives responsible to a board of directors, buy and sell shares on the world's stock exchanges, exercising their judgement as to what will be a profitable investment. Just like any other public company, they make profits and incur losses, and pay dividends to shareholders. Because their companies have assets, investment trust executives can borrow against those assets, and are able to take both a long– and a short-term view of the money entrusted to them. Capital gains on share trading are not distributed in cash but used to build up portfolios and, through the kindness of the Chancellor of the Exchequer, escape taxation.

Investment trusts in Britain now have over almost £20bn. of investors' funds, and Raymond Cazalet, the chairman of the Association of Investment Trust companies, proudly proclaims that most trusts have outperformed the *Financial Times*-Actuaries All Share Index, as well as unit trusts and building society accounts.

Investment trusts are cheaper to invest in than unit trusts. As stated earlier, for every £1,000 invested in unit trusts, it costs £50 in an initial management charge. The same amount used to purchase shares in an investment trust would incur less than £30 in stockbroker's commission and government stamp duty. Unit trust managers also charge an annual fee of between 0.75 to 1.0 per cent for looking after their trusts; investment trust management charges are much lower.

So why do average investors not flock to investment trusts? The answer lies, again, in that word the City prefers not to use about itself – hype. Unit trusts are prolific advertisers in the financial press, and therefore get much more than their fair share of space in the editorial columns. By contrast, investment trusts are restricted by law in their advertising, and get very little press attention. The serious newspapers provide free space to unit trusts to publicize their prices, acknowledging it a public service to do so, but provide only limited price information on investment trusts, whose trade association has to take space itself once a month in *The Financial Times* and *The Daily Telegraph* to provide full statistical information.

Managed Funds

The final group of large institutional investors are different again. These are professional fund management groups, which manage, at their own discretion, the money of others, both individuals and companies. Here again there are similarities with previous groups.

At one end of the scale, there are large stockbroking companies, which take in funds from individuals who either cannot be bothered or feel they lack the expertise to watch the market. These individuals, which range from pensioners in Worthing to wealthy Arabs in Dubai, entrust sums of money – the minimum is usually at least £10,000 – to fund managers within broking houses who manage their portfolio, and keep them posted, through a quarterly or half yearly report, as to what they have done with it. Only rarely would a fund manager consult a client about the purchase or sale of an investment, though most of them are receptive to suggestions. Many broking firms' fund management teams invest in unit trusts and investment trusts, and some have portfolios that stipulate such a limitation.

Some broking houses charge for this service; others rely for income on the commission obtained through sale and purchase of shares, or from a percentage paid to them by unit trusts. This itself can lead to conflict of interest. Those brokers that leave an investment undisturbed are obviously going to benefit less than those that are constantly trading their customer's portfolio, and on many occasions there is much to be said for sticking with the status quo.

At the other end of the scale are the large fund management groups, often a major branch or department of a well-known merchant bank. The principle is the same as with small portfolio management by brokers, but their clients are usually foreign potentates and other very large clients for whom they also act as investment bankers.

The funds under their stewardship are usually measured in billions. For instance, in 1985 Baring Brothers and Co. Ltd managed funds of more than £2,500m., just over half of it in Britain, with clients as diverse as Bowater Corporation, London Transport and London University. More than twice as large, in fund management terms, is Robert Fleming

Investment Management Ltd, with £5,800m. of clients' money to invest, including some of the funds of the Royal National Lifeboat Institution, IBM, Dow Chemical, and Whitbread. Recently Flemings have pushed hard with some success to manage the vast pool of money in the Japanese pension funds.

Other big fund managers include GT Management, £2,000m. with the BBC as a client, Hambros Investment Management, £1,300m., Hill Samuel £3,800m., Lazard Securities, £1,350m., Montague Investment Management, £1,422m., Phillips and Drew £3,000m., J. Henry Schroder Wagg and Co., £4,100m., N. M. Rothschild Asset Management Ltd, £2,500m., and Warburg Investment Management, £4,280m. The biggest seems to be Morgan Grenfell and Co. Ltd, with £6,500m. and blue-chip clients like Ford Motors, Allied Lyons, British Telecom, Plessey and Texas Instruments, and large benevolent funds like the RYAL Air Force Benevolent Society and the Royal National Institution for the Blind.

For all of these groups fund management means a lot more than sitting in a City office, reading research reports, and studying the prices on the electronic monitors. The good fund manager needs to have the judgement of Solomon, the speed of decision-making of a track bookmaker, an ability to size up a balance sheet in minutes, the nose for news of a good newspaper editor, and an eye on the main chance.

With intense competition, both to sell and to perform, and round-the-clock trading, the active fund manager can only grow old in the job if he or she is prepared to put work above everything. It is a long way from the days when the investment manager of the Pru' would make his way back to his office from a lunch at the club to place an investment of £1m. in the British Motor Corporation.

The Fund of Funds

Late in 1985 came a new development – the fund of funds, designed to minimize risk for the small investor and to remove him one further stage away from direct purchases of shares. Instead of having to pick and choose between 800 unit trusts, the investor could buy units in a master fund, which in turn would buy units in one or more of its subsidiary funds. From the point of view of someone with a small amount of capital to invest – but no clear idea if and when to move out of a British equity trust and into a Japanese, German or American one – the fund of funds seems no bad idea. Let someone else do the worrying and save yourself the expense of having a stockbroker to manage a portfolio of unit trusts.

Like most bright ideas, the notion was not a new one. The fund of funds first obtained notoriety as a promotion in 1962 of the international investment swindler Bernie Cornfeld, whose misdeeds are well spelt out in a brilliant book *Do You Sincerely Want To Be Rich*? by Charles Raw, Bruce Page and Godfrey Hodgson. This cautionary tale should be required reading for both investors and all those involved in the financial services industry. As the authors say:

> The salesman's rationale for the Fund of Funds was an unusually owlish piece of nonsense – one of those things that sounds impressive until you really think it through. Mutual funds, and all investment concerns, are sold on the proposition that the ordinary man needs investment advisers to make choices for him. The Fund of Funds went further and suggested that the ordinary man now needed professionals to choose the professionals who would make the choices. The Fund of Funds would take your money, and invest it in other mutual funds – but only in those whose values were rising most rapidly.

A lawyer from the US Securities and Exchange Commission exploded the Fund of Funds argument succinctly:

> If funds of funds are permitted to proliferate, how would an investor decide among the many companies seeking his investment dollar? Would he not need a fund of funds of funds to make this decision?

Cornfeld's Fund of Funds run by his Investors Overseas Services and given the hard-sell by thousands of salesmen calling themselves 'financial counsellors', gathered in $100m. of people's savings within two years of its launch. The customer's money was transferred immediately into separate proprietary funds, for a brokerage fee which was pocketed by IOS. For the privilege of investing at all, the customer had to pay what has become known as a 'front-end load', much of which was used to pay a commission to the salesman who persuaded him to part with his money in the first place. For every $3,000 invested in Cornfeld's Fund of Funds, $540 vanished immediately in fees. A further 10 per cent of any income generated also went in fees, as did 10 per cent of any capital gain. According to Raw, Page and Hodgson an investor had to wait six years before he could even get his money out without loss. An investigation found that money which was supposed to be held on trust for customers was being used for the benefit of IOS itself, its directors, employees and friends; and that the IOS sales force engaged in illegal currency transactions on a major scale, and constantly misrepresented the investment performance of its largest fund.

Whitehall relaxes the rules

The shockwaves that surrounded the fall of IOS were such that the Department of Trade and Industry – which, until 1986, was to rule the unit trust industry with great rigidity – refused point blank to entertain the establishment of any other funds of funds. So adamant were the men in Whitehall that the concept was fraught with danger that few financial institutions bothered to apply for approval of schemes they preferred to call 'managed funds'.

But in the summer of 1985 the respected City broking firm of Grieveson Grant sought DTI approval for the Barrington Planned Investment Trust. Grieveson Grant's rationale was logic itself. According to partner Peter Saunders:

> An increasing number of people are looking for something that is steady if unspectacular, and is not going to risk losing them a great deal of money. The privatization issue, starting with the successful float of British Telecom, the abolition of exchange controls, the much wider use of company share option schemes, and rising property values providing for bigger legacies, has meant that the capital in this country is much more broadly spread, and there are more people with spare capital and savings. We could have stood back and said 'all we are going to do is to

look after people with a quarter of a million pounds or more', but that is not the attitude we are taking.

Had they known about it, Grieveson Grant's rivals in the City might reasonably have expected the DTI to postpone a decision until the full establishment of the new Securities and Investments Board in 1986. But the Whitehall mandarins were prepared to have one last fling. Perhaps now that there were 800 unit trusts, it was argued, it was reasonable to have a fund of funds, to save small investors from the perils of switching. It would also tidy up a small problem over capital gains, for an investor switching from one unit trust to another and making sufficient profit in the process could be liable for capital gains, even though he was only being prudent in transferring an investment from one sector to another. A fund of funds would not be liable for capital gains.

So the Barrington Planned Investment Fund was approved, subject to some tough and, in one case, strange restrictions. An approved fund of funds – the DTI also preferred to call them managed funds – would be restricted in its investments to its manager's own unit trusts, a total contrast with the United States where master funds may invest in anything but their own in-house trusts. The new fund of funds must also be in a group holding at least four subsidiary trusts and not more than 50 per cent of assets can be invested in any one of them. It is allowed to make an initial charge to investors, but cannot charge unit holders a further front-end load when buying into a subsidiary fund. It may also charge double annual management fees.

The DTI decision met considerable criticism, not least from some of Grieveson Grant's major competitors. Some of this can be dismissed as envy, but much of it is justified. The most serious problem with the fund of funds concept, as now authorized, is conflict of interest.

If the manager of a fund of funds is not to upset his colleagues running one of the subsidiary unit trusts in which he must invest, he will have to avoid sudden switching, particularly of very large sums. But if he is not prepared to move in and out of the subsidiary funds as and when he sees fit, he will miss the market opportunities available to those who manage individual portfolios.

Despite these reservations, the fund of funds concept seems here to stay. And if such funds grow in popularity, they have plenty of scope for expansion at the expense of the building societies. One building society alone, the Halifax, controls more than the entire unit trust industry.

The building societies seem likely to be the biggest losers from future growth of the funds. With lower inflation pushing interest rates down, with expensive shopfronts in every High Street, and with large management overheads, they could find it hard to compete, especially as it is no longer essential to invest with a building society in order to obtain a mortgage.

Funds of funds are also likely to be taken up by the life assurance industry. Ever since the Government ceased to allow life assurance or endowment premiums as a tax deduction, removing from life assurance companies a substantial privilege, the flock of commission-remunerated salesmen who have made a living from selling life assurance have had little to sell. Such is the awareness now of the public to the range of more attractive alternative investments available that cold canvassers from the life assurance industry calling on engaged couples or distressed widows have found their job extremely difficult.

Stockbrokers like John Savage of Hoare Govett believe the life assurance industry will be quick to grasp the fund of funds concept. 'There are a lot of intermediaries who really cannot any longer sell their products on investment grounds, and they need a new package to sell. I do not believe these products have been produced to be sold directly to the public. They have been produced for the professional intermediary who has not got a clue about what is going on in the investment world. He is good at selling something. It might be double glazing, it might be insurance bonds, it might be unit trusts, but he has to have a product to sell, and one that will be easily sold on the basis that the client he is selling to won't ask the right questions.'

Michael Russell, from James Capel and Co., agreed that fund of funds would be a new product for life assurance salesmen to sell. He believes, however, that the fund of funds idea does have appeal to new investors – 'the sort of person who had made a few bob out of British Telecom'. 'I do not believe you can knock it', he insisted. 'If you assume that 90 per cent of the people out there have no experience of the stock market, it will be attractive, I would have thought.'

5 Raising Money

Almost every entrepreneur has a dream that he will be able to build up his own business as a private company, and then, because of its success and opportunity for further growth, be able to sell it to the market. For many the happiest solution is to find large numbers of individuals prepared to buy a total stake, of say, 47 per cent, so that the original founder and his family may retain control, while pocketing the cash generated by the sale. The lucky few who do this become instant multi-millionaires, and are still able to hold on to the businesses they started and to run them in much the same way as before.

So how can an entrepreneur use the stock markets for his own benefit? The cardinal rule is that there should be some reason for turning a private company into a public one other than to obtain a personal fortune: indeed it would be very difficult to find members of the Exchange to bring a company to the market if that were seen as the prime purpose.

The most obvious attraction of going public is that obtaining a listing on the London or any other major stock exchange improves the standing of the concern and its products. There are very few manufacturers of branded products or household names that are not public companies or corporations. Even relatively new, and risky, enterprises, such as personal computer manufacturers like Apple Inc., Acorn and Sinclair Research, have accepted the hazards as well as the benefits of being open to full public scrutiny. There are exceptions, of course – one of them is Britain's second airline, British Caledonian – but they are few.

Apart from obtaining a better image, becoming listed on the Stock Exchange also makes it easier, in normal times, to raise finance for expansion and development. Both investors and lenders have a distinct preference for an enterprise that is not the plaything of an individual, or a group of individuals, and even though it is still possible for one man to hold the reins of a large public company, there are many more checks and balances than on private companies, where clever accountants can play interesting games with the balance sheet. The accounts, and other indicators of performance, of public companies are closely scrutinized by meticulous analysts, who are not afraid to publish adverse comment where they believe it to be merited. Thus most public companies are assessed with one objective – are they good investments? Checking the potential of private companies is not easy, even when they are open to scrutiny; private company accounts are freely available only at Companies' House, and then usually one year in arrears. This alone explains why both institutional and private investors are reluctant to commit large sums to unquoted companies. What happens when the leading figures in a private company die? Their heirs may be hopeless businessmen, or may be forced to sell up part of their holding at an inopportune time in order to pay capital transfer tax. Father may drop dead just as the next recession is approaching: subsequent family feuding and a forced sale could leave the outside investors with little to show for their years of support to the old concern.

Another strong advantage to an expanding business in being publicly listed on the Stock Exchange is that it helps in takeovers. Instead of paying cash for an acquisition, a company can often get away with paying for at least part of the cost by offering a share swap, as in the summer of 1985 when Guinness offered shareholders in Bell, the whisky distiller, paper worth considerably more than the market price of their own scrip. When an efficient company is taking over a dull one, shareholders of the latter are often only too glad of the chance of just such an easy escape route.

A final advantage of obtaining a Stock Exchange listing is that the company attracts unsolicited funds. If they think you are doing well, any number of investors will buy your shares. Regular mention in the financial pages is useful publicity and, in the case of well-run companies, makes for easier relations with customers and helps when attempting to attract executive staff.

Going Public

When a company decides it would like to go public, it normally approaches a firm of stockbrokers through its accountants or bankers. There is then the inevitable City lunch, a getting-to-know-you session at which little more will be achieved than a general understanding of the nature of the business, and its goals and aspirations. The directors of the company considering a quotation will also get some idea of how, what is almost certainly a long operation, is planned.

Once contact has been established, and a decision in principle made, a partner in the firm of brokers will seek a total brief on the company – particularly its management structure, and strengths and weaknesses, its labour force, its present shareholders, its competitors, and, of course, a detailed study of full sets of accounts for the previous five years. Quite often this study will show that a Stock Exchange quote is out of the question. With investors and fund managers spoilt for choice, and with the British Government offloading billions of pounds worth of assets in state enterprises, any company that does not offer first-class prospects will not attract support. To go down the road towards a listing, and to issue a prospectus, and then have to withdraw it, would be a costly mistake.

Assuming, however, that the feasibility study shows the prospect of success, the next stage for the stockbroker is to visit the company and its major plants or operations and to see it at work. This will usually be carried out by a senior member of the firm, under the supervision of a partner. The staff member will also try and visit competitors of the company, to seek another assessment, although the need for strict confidentiality makes this aspect of the study difficult. A firm of accountants, not the company's own auditors, will also be commissioned to carry out a thorough investigation.

All this will have to be done within three months, if a reasonable target for a listing is to be achieved. The next step is for the brokers to prepare a detailed proposal for the flotation, which will, in effect, form the blueprint for the day-by-day march towards the listing. The broker will suggest a price band within which shares might be offered – the decision on a firm price will come much later – and will set out a list of financial requirements which will have to be met and propose under-writers, who, at a substantial discount on price, will agree to purchase any shares if the float is undersubscribed. The company will usually be asked to pay off all major loans – for no investor is keen on picking up a load of debt – and to revalue all properties.

This stage completed, the next step is to decide how the capital of the company is to be made available to the public. In most cases, this will be through the issue of a prospectus, offering the shares at a price expected to be lower than the price at which the company will start its life on the Stock Exchange boards. Usually such a prospectus is published in full in *The Financial Times*, and, occasionally, other newspapers. The prospectus is, in fact, an offer for sale. It will detail the price at which shares will be available, and name any proposed restrictions on voting rights. The terms of sale will be set out, as well as the names and addresses of the auditors, stockbrokers, bankers, solicitors and directors. There will be a full description of the business, a potted history, and a detailed description of its products or services.

Isotron, a company providing the only independent gamma radiation service in Britain, published just such a prospectus in July 1985. It devoted thousands of words to an extremely detailed description of its technological processes, and its business prospects. A large part of the prospectus was devoted to the curricula vitae of the directors and senior employees, right down to site managers. There was a chapter on safety procedures, while over a page of closely-spaced print was devoted to publication of the independent report by accountants Peat, Marwick, Mitchell and Co. The reader was spared no detail, and the prospectus constituted an extremely thorough insight into the company.

Once the prospectus has been written, usually by the merchant bankers advising the company in association with the stockbrokers, the approval of the Quotations Committee of the Stock Exchange must be sought. This is much more than a formality, and it is quite normal for members of the Committee to raise questions on matters of detail. The most pressing concern of the Exchange's Quotations Department is to see that the prospectus gives as full and accurate a picture as possible of the company and its prospects, and it is unlikely that a document will pass through unamended. Once the Stock Exchange has approved the prospectus, a copy must be sent to the Registrar of Companies for the public record.

The terms of sale vary widely. Sometimes an underwriting firm of brokers will agree to buy all the share capital to be offered for sale on a given day, and then do their best to dispose of the shares to investors at a sufficiently higher price to offer them a profit. Sometimes the shares will be offered directly to the public by advertisement; where this happens the underwriters will only have to take on the shares left unsold, and if the issue is a success, may end up with no commitment and a useful underwriting fee.

Finding an underwriter is usually not a major problem, for all brokers have a list of those they can call upon, whether institutions, unit trusts, merchant banks or other financial groups. Underwriters do count, however, on the integrity and accuracy of a broker's recommendation. No firm of brokers can consider accepting the job of arranging a flotation unless it is convinced it is a sound investment.

An increasingly popular way of raising the cash is through public tender – used by bankers J. Henry Schroder Wagg and Co. in the Isotron case mentioned earlier. Here 3,290,088 ordinary 25p. shares were offered at a minimum tender price of 120p. a share, the system being that those prepared to offer a higher rate would receive the biggest allocation. Having received all the applications, Schroders were left with the task of setting a 'striking price', not exceeding the highest price at which sufficient applications were received to cover the total number of shares offered. A public tender was also used by Schroder's and Phillips and Drew in bringing Andrew Lloyd Webber's Really Useful Group to a full Stock Exchange listing in January 1986.

Obviously public tender is a system favoured by highly successful, confident and relatively well-known companies. It is not to be recommended if oversubscription is thought unlikely. It also avoids 'stagging' – a stag being the individual who buys new issues in the confident belief that oversubscription will lead to the price rising sharply on the day of listing.

Whether stagging occurs in the majority of cases when the

tender system is not used depends, of course, very much upon the price at which the shares are fixed for sale. Pricing can be the key to the whole issue. If prices are pitched too low, there will be a huge oversubscription, involving vast amounts of extra paperwork, the return of cheques, and the difficult job of selecting the lucky applicants to receive shares. The stags will have a field day. If, at the other extreme, the price is pitched too high, the issue will be a disaster, and months, even years, of work will be wasted. There have been examples of both, and where there is oversubscription, those applicants left out, or, as in the case of the Britoil issue, awarded derisory holdings, feel aggrieved, even bitter.

Fixing the price is not easy, however, because all companies are the prisoners of current events. A series of air crashes could damage the price of the shares of a manufacturer of jet engines, for instance. Inevitably setting the price is left to almost the last possible moment, with brokers and bankers using their experience to judge market conditions as D-Day approaches. The forty days and forty nights before and after the day of flotation are the busiest, when near frenzy envelops the offices of those directly involved. It is not unusual for the major people involved to camp in their offices during much of this period, and certainly holidays are out of the question. While the final offer documents are away at the printers, they just pray that they have got it right.

Whether a company goes public through a full float or sale by tender, it is a costly business. The experts needed – lawyers, merchant bankers, accountants, brokers, and financial public relations men – do not come cheap, especially in the City. There are few ways of doing it cheaper, but one of them is to arrange what is called a placement. In this case, the stockbrocking firm buys all the shares and sells them direct to its clients, avoiding the cost of dealing. This method is used in small new issues, or where there is unlikely to be much public interest. But even here, the Stock Exchange regulations stipulate that at least 35 per cent of the company's issued capital must be in the placement, thereby preventing directors from using the system as a ploy to pick up some useful cash while still totally dominating the company. At least one-quarter of the shares must also be sold to the public on the stock markets, so that market makers set a price, which helps when open dealings start. A placement is much cheaper because the costs of advertising, printing and professional services will be much less, and there is no need for underwriters.

There is also the alternative of arranging an introduction, but this way of obtaining a quotation on the London Stock Exchange is only available to those companies that already have a wide distribution of shareholders, and where there is no immediate intention of anyone selling out. No capital is offered prior to listing, and it is therefore not necessary for the company to go through the procedures described earlier, or to issue a prospectus, although it is required to take an advertisement to publicize the move. This method is most commonly used when a large foreign company decides to have its shares listed in London as well as on its home exchange.

Raising More Money

The Stock Exchange was founded to raise money for industry and to provide finance for great national projects such as railways and canals. It raised money with great success until World War II, and in the early post-war years it was the place where companies went for extra funds if they wanted to expand. Borrowing from the banks was, in Britain at least, considered expedient only for short-term finance. Borrowing from overseas – through instruments such as Eurobonds, and more recently ECU-denominated Eurobonds and Euronotes – was not even in the minds of those few City types who supported Jean Monnet's vision of an integrated European economic community. Raising money was the job of the Stock Exchange. Why go further than Throgmorton Street?

Things began to go badly wrong with the capital-raising function of the Stock Exchange when successive governments, mostly, but not exclusively, of Socialist persuasion, decided that the best way of paying for expensive public programmes was to soak the rich, which, to them, included almost everyone who did not belong to a trade union and pick up his wages in a brown envelope once a week. Income from share ownership was 'unearned income', and somehow thought of as less decent than interest obtained from a building society. Making a capital gain by selling one's own shares at a profit in order to pay for old age, school fees, or even a trip to the Bahamas, was regarded as sinful, and therefore had to be discouraged through extra taxation. Company taxes were raised, making it harder for businesses to fund expansion. And, in order to justify an ill-judged attempt to curb a free market for wages, 'dividend restraint' was imposed. With little point in investing either for capital growth or for income, investors followed the example of the trade union movement, and went on strike. In other words, they ceased buying shares, and held on to their holdings in such lame ducks as British Leyland, Dunlop, and Alfred Herbert, and watched them gradually run out of capital.

The political effect of the onslaught on the investor in the 1960s and 1970s was to bring to an almost complete halt a Stock Exchange system which allowed development capital to be raised, pluralistically, by a large number of individuals and institutions, and to replace it by a more costly system of finance through banks. It seems unlikely that the trend will ever be completely reversed, but in recent years there has been an encouraging revival of capital-raising on the Stock Exchange, to the benefit of both saver and entrepreneur.

This is usually done through a rights issue, and in the 1980s there have been several companies who have enjoyed a spectacular expansion of their capital base by such a method. Perhaps the most noteworthy example is Hanson Trust plc, which was first listed on the Stock Exchange in 1964. Since then there have been several rights issues, the most recent, in 1985, raising over £500m. enabling the company to bid for a leading American manufacturer. An investor buying 100 shares in Hanson Trust in 1964 could scarcely have expected that over the next 21 years he would be called upon to stump up an extra £1.36m. But had he done so – and some have – those shares would now be worth a cool £50m.

What happens with a rights issue is that the holders of ordinary shares in a company are offered further shares at a discount, usually substantial enough to make it attractive. Under the rules, such new shares must be offered to existing stockholders in quantities proportionate to their holdings. In case not all shareholders are willing, or even able, to take up the rights offer, underwriters have to be found who will. At the time of writing the Chancellor of the Exchequer was among those supporting change, so that large British companies can raise additional capital directly from new shareholders rather than through traditional rights issues. As with new issues, pitching the price right is crucial. If a rights issue is undersubscribed there is a danger that the share price will fall, even if underwriters have been appointed, and this would defeat part of the objective of the exercise, which is to raise more capital. In the case of the 1985 Hanson Trust rights issue, the event was not without drama, and the Kuwait Investment Office obligingly took up the shares that some of the company's shareholders did not want.

An alternative to a rights issue is loan capital, which may be raised on the Stock Exchange either through unsecured loan stock or convertible stock. Loan stock is usually issued only by blue-chip companies; a company without a high rating would not find investors ready to buy it even at very high interest rates, and provide for the holder to convert all or some of the shares at a later stage to equities.

If a company is planning to modernize its plant to increase output and productivity, loan capital can be a particularly attractive vehicle. The interest paid is deductible before corporation tax is payable, so the company's tax bill is reduced. And as output rises, and hopefully profits, so does the company's share price, making it beneficial for the shareholders to make the conversion.

As with new issues, there are several ways in which a stockbroker can obtain loan capital for his clients. He can arrange for a full prospectus detailing the offer to be prepared, published and advertised, and wait for the response, usually stipulating preferential treatment to existing shareholders. He may, if he chooses, place the loan stock with institutions direct – unlike placements with new issues, where a proportion has to be offered on the Stock Exchange. Or he may limit the offer to existing shareholders, an unlikely course because especially attractive terms are usually necessary to get full support. A placement is usually much more efficient.

Then there is the bond market, of which the Eurobond

market is the best known. Not long ago, only governments of stable and prosperous democracies and large international institutions such as the World Bank and the European Investment Bank would go to the bond market for funds, by issuing securities at good interest rates with maturity dates 10 to 20 years away. Mostly denominated in dollars, these securities offered large institutional investors an attractive hedge against the fall of sterling and against inflation, but the mainstays of the market were in fact Belgian professional people who found bonds a particularly good alternative to other investments in their own country.

There is no specific building or exchange for the Eurobond market. The bonds are bought and sold by licensed bond dealers, which include major London stockbroking firms and merchant banks, and trading is all conducted on the telephone, with the dealers themselves cooperating to maintain a list of prices.

The Eurobond markets enjoyed spectacular expansion in the late 1970s and early 1980s, as international banks and treasurers of large corporations grasped the fact that their names were often as good as governments in securing support. They were aided by the vast pool of investors' money awash in the Euromarkets, including that belonging to those who saw no reason to repatriate it to their home country and who were anxious to diversify their portfolios beyond national frontiers. Both the American and Japanese pension funds have recently adopted investment policies allowing for international diversification, and the bond market is a secure way of achieving that goal.

In 1980 a handful of French and Italian companies hit upon the idea of using international bonds denominated in the European Currency Unit, an artificial currency used to reflect the value of the nine currencies of the European Community, weighted according to their size and importance. ECU bonds, by the nature of the differences between the major economies in the EC, offer the strength and security of the Deutschemark plus higher interest than D-Mark bonds because of the higher volatility of some of the EC's more precarious economies. 'It was the individual, conservative Belgian investor – the Belgian dentist – who bought them', Pierre Jaegly, Manager of Cedel, the Eurobond clearing house in Luxembourg told me. 'ECU bonds gave them higher yields than on D-mark bonds, but still had stability.'

As US Investors looked for diversification out of the dollar, the popularity of ECU bonds as a hedge against the currency increased, and more and more companies looked to this method for capital-raising. By 1985, the ECU was running a close second to the Deutschemark as the most important currency for new Eurobond issues after the dollar. Besides government issues, industrial giants like Chrysler, Philips and Fiat raised funds in ECUs, along with more glamorous names such as Walt Disney and Club Méditerranée.

More recently there has been the development of Eurobonds denominated in other currencies, particularly the Australian dollar and the Japanese yen. An insight into the strength of the Eurobond market can be gained by looking at the new issues in two currencies, the Swiss franc and the Japanese yen, in one week in August 1985 – traditionally a quiet month. Five Japanese companies raised a total of 600m. Swiss francs, at interest rates averaging 3 per cent. In the same week in the yen market eight European and American companies raised 210bn. yen, at interest rates averaging 8 per cent.

Then there is another new market – syndicated international equity issues. In the three years 1983-5 the market for these was worth $2.2bn., with companies issuing new shares on average every three weeks. Almost all the companies involved were household names, like Thomson-CSF and Michelin of France, Nestlé of Switzerland, and Alcan Aluminium and Bell from Canada, but only two British companies, British Telecom and Britoil, made significant use of the market during that period. More than 70 per cent of the business is controlled by two US investment banks, Morgan Stanley and Crédit Suisse First Boston; a Japanese broker, Nomura Securities; and the Swiss Bank Corporation. London had less than 4 per cent of the business through one bank, S. G. Warburg.

The Unlisted Securities Market

Money can be raised for small and medium-sized go-ahead businesses through the junior Stock Exchange, better known as the USM, or Unlisted Securities Market. Similar markets have evolved in the United States and France, and the idea has widespread political support because such businesses are seen as major sources of job-creation, technological innovation and entrepreneurship. The high-interest rate environment of the past few years has compounded the financing problems of the growing company, but the USM does offer those who have a case and can present it well the chance not only of raising capital for their expansion, but also of becoming rich in the process.

In essence, joining the Unlisted Securities Market, which was only established in 1980, is a much simpler procedure than going for a full listing, but with many similarities. The cost is also much less – £50,000 for a medium-sized company with no major problems – and companies need only have had a three-year trading record.

The most common way of going to the USM is via a brokers' placing, whereby shares are sold directly by brokers to their customers, although 25 per cent have to be offered on the open market. A company seeking to join the USM discusses the prospect with his accountant, who mounts a thorough investigationn into its affairs, and produces a prospectus. The most crucial factor in joining the USM is timing, since there are more capital seekers than funds available. If, during the one-year march towards a float, the company's financial advisers notice any downturn in prospects, they will almost certainly urge postponement.

More than 350 companies are now traded on the USM, valued at more than £3.6bn. The USM has been of great benefit to a number of businesses, but it has not exactly been a Mecca for investors. An excellent investigation by Lucy Kellaway of *The Financial Times* found that, of the first 11 companies to join the USM, all but three were either trading below their issue prices, or had been taken over at depressed levels. But the three winners, Fuller and Smith brewers, London and Continental Advertising, and McLaughlin and Harvey builders had tripled their investment. London and

Continental was the real success story, for it was able to use its funding to buy London and Provincial Posters, two and a half times its size, for £20m., an acquisition which increased its turnover from posters eightfold, and enabled it to obtain a full listing. On the other hand, weighed down by three poorly-performing oil companies in the list, anyone who put £100 into the first eleven in November 1980 would be left with only £40 five years later.

6 The Takeover Trail

'That's what a dawn raid is. You hit at dawn' – Robert Holmes à Court.

'The old gentlemanly way of doing things is going to disappear. Managements and their advisers will strain the rules to their legal limits' – David Nash, Acquisitions Manager of ICI.

'It has always to be borne in mind that what seem to be problems today may be dwarfed by the complexities of new types of market operation which are being elaborated for use tomorrow' – Ian Fraser, first Director-General of the Panel on Takeovers and Mergers.

Takeover activity is where the Stock Exchange is at its most exciting. Even uncontested takeovers have strong elements of uncertainty, and where a bid is unwanted by one party, there is usually a sharp battle of wills and wits.

On paper a takeover is simple enough. Since shares are freely traded, any individual or company that can persuade enough shareholders of another company to sell to them can obtain sufficient votes to elect a new board of directors and take control, no matter what the existing directors and management may think. Having obtained control, they may use the assets of the acquired company in any way that does not breach the law. For instance, they may sell these assets. In the 1950s boards and their managerial advisers were so slack in revaluing assets, or making proper use of them, that many companies were laid bare through a process that became known as asset-stripping. Although the work of two generations of asset-strippers has sharpened up directors to the risk, there is still a hard core of professionals who make millions by spotting companies that are undervalued.

There are, however, some rules to the game. Although

they do not have statutory backing and have been rewritten three times since they first appeared as the City Takeover Code in March 1968, they are now enshrined in the litany of self-regulation that accompanies the 1986 Financial Services Act. Their observation is supervised by the City Takeover Panel, a group of twelve City elders whose modest secretariat is based on the twentieth floor of the Stock Exchange building. There is a director-general, two deputies, a secretary, and a few other executives. The permanent staff provide interpretations of the Code, but contested rulings and disciplinary cases are considered by the Panel itself, with the right of appeal to the Appeals Committee, which sits under the chairmanship of a retired Lord of Appeal. The Panel operates under the watchful eye of the Bank of England; it is usual for the majority of its staff to be on secondment from the Bank, providing a constant flow of fresh ideas. Walker-Haworth himself was seconded from merchant bankers S. G. Warburg.

The most important rule is that you may bid for up to 29.9 per cent of a company's shares before launching a full bid, but after that you must make a full offer for all the remaining shares, at the highest price you have paid for the purchases so far. This is to prevent a predator buying a company on the cheap, especially where there is a wide spread of share ownership.

Another rule provides that before an offer is announced, no one privy to the preliminary takeover or merger discussions is allowed to deal in the shares of either the bidding or target company. Once an offer is announced, the share transactions in all the companies involved must be reported by all parties to the City Takeover Panel, the Stock Exchange, and the Press. Companies defending a bid must not do anything without shareholder approval 'which could effectively result in any bona fide offer being frustrated, or in the shareholders of the offeree company being denied an opportunity to decide on its merits'.

The City Takeover Panel's executive staff are available throughout a takeover to advise whether the rules are in danger of being broken, as all bids for public companies, listed or unlisted, are strictly monitored. The staff work closely with the surveillance unit at the Stock Exchange to investigate dealings in advance of publication of bid proposals, the aim being to establish whether there has been any breach of the rules governing secrecy and abuse of privileged information.

If there appears to have been a breach of the code, the Panel staff invite the chairman of the company involved, or other individuals, to appear before the Panel. He or she is informed by letter of the nature of the alleged breach, and of the matters which the director-general will present to the hearing. These hearings are informal, there are no rules of evidence, and, although notes are taken, no permanent records are kept. The principal against whom the complaint has been made is expected to appear in person, although he may bring his lawyer with him. At the hearing he is expected to set out his reply, normally based on a document which should already have been produced in reply to the director-general's letter. If the Panel finds there has been a breach, the offender may be reprimanded there and then, or may be subjected to public censure with a press release distributed to the media, setting out the Panel's conclusions and its reasons for them. In a bad case, where the Panel feels that the offender should no longer be able to use the Stock Exchange temporarily or permanently, the case may be referred to a professional association, the Stock Exchange, the Department of Trade and Industry, or the City Fraud Squad.

The Panel is considered to be a legal entity, and the Court of Appeal has ruled that its decisions may, if need be, be reviewed by the Courts.

Making an Acquisition

Before considering how a takeover works, it is perhaps worth analysing some of the many and varied reasons for making an acquisition. The most obvious is that it is usually much easier and cheaper than starting a new business, except in the case of a product or service that is exclusive enough to depend, for its success, on the professional drive and energy of the entrepreneur and his team. If you have a product that will put your rivals out of business, you will usually be best served by building up the business yourself.

But if you wish to expand a business, a takeover is a useful route. Apart from anything else, it often enables you to use other people's money to achieve your ambition. A takeover can be a way of swallowing up the competition, and thereby increasing profit margins, although the Government has the Monopolies and Mergers Commission to attempt to frustrate just such an ambition.

In many cases, a takeover may appear to be the only way to fulfil ambitions of growth. Sometimes a takeover may be the result of egomania on the part of the chairman or controlling shareholder; there is never a shortage of new owners for Fleet Street newspapers, for instance, or for prestigious department stores, and breweries also seem popular. Sometimes the thrust of a takeover effort is to achieve a lifetime ambition, such as the attempt by Lord Forte and his son Rocco to gain control of the Savoy Hotel in London, an attempt that has always been thwarted by the antiquated and inefficient method of issuing preference shares.

Whatever the reason, there are usually only two forms of takeover: those that are uncontested, and those that involve a fight. But it is never as simple as that. There have been many occasions when a board of directors has decided to open merger discussions with a potential target rather than to proceed by stealth, only to find that the opposition is so great that all they have achieved is to give the other side advance warning to prepare for an assault. And there have been occasions when a contested battle has been so fierce and the cost of the operation so high that it might have been better to attempt to achieve the same result through negotiation.

Some takeovers are solicited. Many a company, for lack of progress or good management, feels that it would be better served if it were to be incorporated in a better run, and perhaps larger, business. I was once a non-executive director of a small public company in the retail motor trade. It had garages as far-flung as South Wales, Southampton, Birmingham and Lincolnshire, with different franchises in each. In one period of three months the Thatcher Government lifted interest rates three percentage points, thereby forcing the sale of stocked used cars at giveaway prices; an oil company decided not to renew the lease on the premises with the best showroom because they wanted a larger forecourt for petrol sales; and a strike at Vauxhall Motors dried up the supply of new cars for valuable orders at the main dealership. The directors, rightly I believe, sought to merge our company with a larger group better able to sit out what was to become a four-year crisis for the motor trade, and entered into discussions with a number of potential buyers. At one stage we were close to a deal. But then our shares slipped in the market; our creditors, seeing our market capitalization falling and rightly assuming that interest bills were rising, pressed harder, and the banks called in the receivers. The irony is that had it been a private company, without a listing, the company could well have weathered the storm, for the shareholders would have been obliged to stick with it through the bad times. Directors, of course, were not allowed to sell out, nor could they tell those friends who had supported the company, because that would have been classed as one of the most serious City offences, insider trading, punishable by heavy fines or imprisonment. So those that had risked their livelihoods lost their shirt. It seemed rough justice at the time, but does illustrate an important point made earlier: the shareholders in a public company are much better protected than those in a private one.

There may also be hidden hazards in a solicited takeover. Take the case of Sinclair Research, a company built up by a technological wizard, Sir Clive Sinclair, credited with building the world's smallest portable television set, and the designer of an all-British range of microcomputers. Sinclair's drive and technological brillance were not matched, however, by management skills, and many of his investments, such as his battery-operated vehicle, were less than successful.

In 1983, four years after it was founded, Sinclair Research had a market capitalization of £136m. In 1983 and 1984 the company was turning in profits of about £14m., and in 1985, although market conditions turned down due to a slump in the personal computer market, it was still looking to a useful profit. But in May of that year, serious cash flow problems became evident as stocks of £35m. of unsold goods built up, with suppliers demanding payment of their bills. For a while the main creditors, Thorn EMI and Timex of Dundee, agreed to hold off, and Sinclair's bankers, Barclays and Citicorp, increased the company's borrowing facilities. But, almost inevitably, the crunch came, and Sinclair turned to the bear-like clutches of Robert Maxwell, publisher of Mirror Group Newspapers, who, for reasons which have never been made very clear, made a £12m. rescue bid for Sinclair Research. Two months later, on 9 August 1985, it was all off. Maxwell announced that he was pulling out, saying the deal 'just did not gell', though he had no doubt that Sinclair computers were a 'fine product appreciated by millions'. Sir Clive Sinclair put a brave face on it, smiled wanly, and went off to see his creditors. It is a salutary lesson for those who see a takeover as salvation: you have to be sure you are really wanted.

With any takeover there are two stages: the preliminaries, which may take weeks and even months, and the active stage, when the bid is made and the offer digested and voted upon by the shareholders. Very few takeovers are the result of a whim, but are usually considered only after painstaking research, involving the company's solicitors, accountants and merchant banks, or other financial advisers.

Takeover specialists are at a premium in the City, and are paid enormous salaries. According to one leading firm of headhunters, Michael Paige Associates, a senior director in the corporate finance department of one of the better known British merchant banks may expect to earn about £250,000 a year in salary and bonuses, while a junior director, who could be in his late twenties or early thirties, might receive £70,000 upwards. American companies pay more, but offer marginally less job security. For this, the specialists advise those either making or subject to a takeover on strategy and tactics, capital-raising where necessary, and public relations, often calling in outside specialists to assist. When the pressure is on, as at the end of 1985, most advisers would expect to work 14 hours a day, as well as attending meetings at weekends. If their homes are outside central London, they would be lucky to see their families except at the weekend, and would almost certainly have to stay in hotels close to the City. One merchant bank maintains an apartment for its directors above an expensive West End restaurant. If you are seen, however, dining with a new client, word soon gets out. Takeover advisers have to work under conditions of great secrecy, for an essential part of the takeover game is to anticipate your opponent's next move, and to outwit him.

However, for the merchant bank that can grab the lion's share of the business, the rewards are great, with takeovers and operations in the Euromarkets earning the greatest portion of its income. In 1985 fees from takeover activity probably earned City merchant banks not far short of £200m. There is a scramble to be top dog, and a magazine *Acquisitions Weekly*, now publishes a league table of the winners and losers.

Growth Through Acquisition

Hanson Trust plc, which has grown into Britain's tenth largest company with a market capitalization of £2.5bn., started off selling fertilizers and renting out coal sacks. Much of its growth has been through acquisitions. In its 21-year history as a public company, Hanson Trust has lifted profits steadily from £140,000 to £252m. in 1985. The company maintains full-time senior executives in both Britain and the United States whose sole job is to earmark takeover targets, what one of the directors called 'culling', in other words raking through the performance records of industrial concerns looking for those that would benefit from the rigorous management style developed by the chairman, Lord Hanson, a tough Yorkshireman. Lord Hanson's methods are refreshingly simple. First the head office should be small; in his case a suite in London's Brompton Road, where there are less than 50 executives. Secondly there should be stringent financial controls: the centre operates like a merchant bank, draws in cash from the subsidiaries and insists on referral for expenditures over £1,000. Thirdly, and most important, the central management, including Hanson himself, leave the running of the businesses, which include Ever Ready, the batteries company, London Brick, the Allders stores group and airport duty-free shops, to those on the spot, limiting their own involvement to financial questions. Performance is guaranteed by generous incentive schemes, involving high cash rewards for those who achieve, not the best sales, the best image, or the lowest costs, but the greatest return on capital employed.

Both Lord Hanson and City observers reject any suggestion that Hanson Trust is an asset stripper. 'He does sell off parts of a company he takes over that he does not require', Robert Morton, an analyst with Barclays DeZoete Wedd told me, 'but that is because he knows what he wants, and there is no point in keeping the bits he does not want.'

During takeovers it is normal for managements of the 'losing' side to be replaced, and during the great insurance company mergers of the 1950s even clerical staffs feared redundancy, or a future with very little hope. This has now changed to some degree, and many acquisitions are made on the basis that the staff of the comapny acquired are guaranteed a job, and only top management are axed. This is the system operated by Hanson Trust. According to BZW's Morton:

> Board level moves on, and those lower in the company move up and benefit from the new incentives. Only very seldom does Lord Hanson go outside an acquired company for executives, normally finding there are people in the lower ranks who are pretty good.

In planning a takeover, it is essential to work out a strategy before going public. This usually means weeks closeted with financial advisers, and is a time when security is all-important. A stray document left in a photocopying machine, a loose word dropped to a friend in a bar, or even incautious lunching can lead to a leak. One paragraph in a newspaper can be enough to set the takeover target's shares racing ahead on the Stock Exchange, which could rule a bid out, or alert rivals to the possibility.

As in a war, strategy is the key. There is no better example of a well-thought out takeover strategy than the recent successful £356m. bid for Bell, the Scotch whisky distiller, by Guinness, the brewer. If one was to believe the Guinness propaganda campaign, Bell was a company less than completely run, in urgent need of salvation. The truth was a little different. Arthur Bell and Co. manufactured one of Britain's most successful and distinctive products, Bell's whisky, as well as having a number of other useful assets. It was fiercely proud of its Scottish roots, and had enjoyed a ten-year record of unbroken growth of profits and dividends. It was, in no sense, a company needing help. Whatever the Guinness board may have said, they knew this only too well, and therefore spent 18 months preparing themselves for a long and bitter battle. It was not enough just to study Bell's balance sheet; Guinness needed to know all there was to know about the whisky business, for it is a ferociously competitive one, with some of the rival and best known brands, such as Johnny Walker and Teachers, in the hands of large groups like Allied Lyons. The Monopolies Commission would not, of course, permit a bid by Allied had one even been contemplated, but Guinness had to be sure they could run Bell's at least as well as the existing owners.

Furthermore, takeover strategy these days is not confined merely to obtaining enough shares in the targeted concern. In almost every situation, politics and public relations come to the fore. In some cases, they take precedence: for example, when United Newspapers, a medium-sized publisher of provincial newspapers with no national newspaper of its own, wanted to bid for Fleet Newspapers, publishers of the *Daily Express* and *Sunday Express*, it had first to seek the permission of the Monopolies Commission. It was even deemed impolitic to indicate a price, so Fleet shareholders had to play a guessing game for months.

This was also true with the Guinness bid for Bell. Guinness was fortunate in having, as its financial adviser, the Morgan Grenfell merchant bank, acknowledged as one of the best in the takeover field, and Cazenove and Company, the preeminent stockbroking experts in corporate finance, who wisely also employed another large firm of stockbrokers, Wood Mackenzie and Co., who had Scottish origins, a large Scottish base, and in-depth research knowledge of the whisky industry. They quickly reported that an analysis of the Bell shareholders' register revealed that London institutional shareholders were among the main investors, and control could probably be won in the City. But Guinness also had to be able to count on political support, both in Westminster and in Scotland, where independence aspirations run strong. It therefore sought the advice of Sir Gordon Reece, the media consultant, and appointed Edinburgh's leading merchant bank, Noble Grossart, to act on its behalf, and to be ready to reassure Scottish interests when the time came for the shouting to begin.

Despite, perhaps because of, all these preparations, word emerged that someone was sniffing around at Arthur Bell and Co. and on 13 June 1985 there was a sharp rise in the Bell share price. At this point the Bell board made a fatal mistake. The chairman, Raymond Miquel, was out of the country on a business trip to the United States. When a takeover bid appears imminent, it is essential for the captain to be on the bridge, and Miquel erred in not catching the overnight flight from Chicago to London. The next day Guinness swooped. In a short statement to the Stock Exchange it announced a £327m. bid. For five days Miquel remained in Chicago, occasionally taking telephone calls and condemning the offer. On his return to Britain, he then made what was perhaps another mistake; he held a press conference, not in Edinburgh, but in London's Hilton Hotel, waiting until the following day to repeat the message for disgruntled but influential Scottish journalists.

Guinness, by contrast, had played it clever. The Guinness bid was timed for late Friday, always a good time for a takeover bid. Advised by Broad Street Associates, a City financial public relations firm whose managing director, Bryan Basham, had been a veteran of many successful takeovers, including the successful bid by the Egyptian Al Fayed brothers for the House of Fraser, Ernest Saunders, Guinness's chief executive, devoted most of Friday evening and Saturday to briefing financial journalists and stockbroking analysts, insisting that the offer was both logical and likely to succeed. He had a receptive audience, and was rewarded with substantial favourable publicity in the Sunday newspapers. But even before he had read the results of these efforts, Saunders caught the British Airways shuttle to Edinburgh, and on Sunday was available in his hotel ready to face the probings of inquisitive Scottish journalists and brokers anxious to discover what might happen to their beloved whisky company under Guinness ownership. Saunders won several friends on that trip, and it was his frequent returns to Edinburgh as the battle intensified over succeeding weeks that played no small part in creating the atmosphere that led to a majority of Bell's shareholders accepting the offer.

While Saunders had gained the upper hand for Guinness, Bell was floundering. When the offer had been delivered to its head office in Perth, its directors discovered that the firm they thought was its merchant bank in such matters, Morgan Grenfell, was acting for Guinness. Four days later it lodged a formal complaint to the City Takeover Panel, and sought legal advice as to whether it could sue. It was a lost cause. Morgan's pointed out that it had not been asked to act for Bell for 18 months, and noted that the whisky company was also consulting another merchant bank, Henry Ansbacher. (It is not unusual for a company to have more than one merchant bank, just as individuals often maintain more than one bank account.) Bell also did not have a financial public relations firm with the expertise of Broad Street Associates at the end of a telephone, and its brokers also lacked the nous of Cazenove and Co.

It was almost one week after the bid before Bell's board was able to swing into action. A strong political supporter, Bill Walker, Tory MP for Tayside, made representations to the Office of Fair Trading that it should block the Guinness bid. The OFT rejected his advice. Miquel, back in Perth, jetted up and down to London, working on Bell's defence. Finally, on 25 June, 11 days after the bid, Bell appointed a City heavyweight, merchant bankers S. G. Warburg and Co., to act on its behalf.

For the Guinness team, this indicated that the struggle was far from over. Warburg's reputation as defendants on the takeover chess board was as good as Morgan Grenfell's was for attack. Guinness moved to stage two – a £1m. advertising campaign in the press unlike anything seen in any previous takeover campaign. Readers of *The Financial Times*, accustomed to the drabness of tombstone advertisements, were suddenly treated each breakfast time to black headlines two inches tall. 'Bell's on the Rocks?', said one, above a telling graph comparing the company's relative share performance with the FT-Actuaries All Share Index. The Bell share price graph showed a sharp fall, and the accompanying copy said, 'Shareholders are now paying the price of the failure of Bell's management to tackle its problems. Even in its latest defence document, the board of Bell's has given no indication that it recognizes that problems exist, let alone has plans to overcome them.'

Bell's responded with its own full-page advertisements. The type size even larger, and the language as vituperative, but the advertisements lacked the panache of those placed by Morgan Grenfell on behalf of Guinness. 'Bell's has growth potential, Bell's is a sound investment', one advertisement proclaimed. 'Ignore the Guinness slogans. Guinness' publicity marks its basic weakness in business and management methods.'

Guinness, and its financial advisers, were not going to take this lying down. Each day Saunders and his aides met to dream up more slogans, occasionally using the 'Guinness is good for you' slogan which the company had not been permitted to use for product advertising because it could not prove its truth. In the case of financial advertising, no such proof was required. 'Will your Bell's shares ever be worth as much to you again?', asked a new advertisement, containing just one message – 'before the 262p. Guinness offer, Bell's shares had stood on the market at only 143p'. A few days later this message was followed up with another, in similar vein: 'How to make your Bell's investment worth 90 per cent more.'

Meanwhile Bell's merchant bankers were doing their best to present Bell as a company with more to offer shareholders under their existing directors than under Saunders. Shortly before midnight on 5 August a second defence document was published, containing an upwardly revised profits forecast, and the pledge of a 66 per cent increase in dividend. In the document, chairman Miquel also said that its refurbished Piccadilly Hotel would soon contribute extra profits.

Once again Guinness was ready with a response. It published further advertisements claiming that Bell's share of the Scotch whisky marker had declined by 20 per cent in the previous five years. It picked up five optimistic statements by Miquel, and ran what it said were 'the facts' in a second column against them.

In other words, good, hard-hitting stuff. But it took real money for Guinness to clinch the deal. It increased its bid, offering Bell shareholders four new ordinary stock plus £2.65

in cash for every five ordinary shares in Bell. It also bought a 3.25 per cent stake in Bell owned by Ladbroke, the gaming and leisure group, which had earlier discussed with Bell the possibility of buying its hotels.

For the shareholders the contest was over. For them the danger had been that failure to accept the Guinness offer would almost certainly have led to the share price drifting sharply back to its earlier lower levels. Much the same fear was at work in another takeover, the bid by Ralph Halpern's Burton Group for the department store chain, Debenhams. Halpern also used the press effectively, by publishing a large blow-up of the Debenham share price of 185p., before the Burton offer. 'Remember the price before we came along?', asked the banner headlines. 'No prizes for guessing where it will go if you allow our offer to lapse.'

The Guinness example indicates how necessary it is for all involved in a takeover – company executives, merchant banks, stockbrokers, accountants and public relations men – to keep on their toes. The predator in a takeover also enjoys one major advantage: it can always count on the full support of its management team, which usually has much to gain from taking charge of a larger organization. By contrast the management of a target company often finds itself in a difficult, even ambivalent, position; its loyalties are to its present board of directors, but its future, as likely as not, will lie elsewhere. It also has the burden of dealing with a worried staff, not to mention suppliers, distributors, and others with whom the company has close connections. And it has to continue to run the business. On the other hand, experience shows that shareholders will tend to stand by a business that has done well by them, unless those making the bid make an irrefutable case. Ralph Halpern of Burton had to fight long and hard and paid dearly for control of Debenhams, whose major shareholders, including its chairman, walked away with a tidy profit.

It is also true that the best defence against a takeover is to act before a bid, rather than afterwards – in other words, take action which will deter a predator from striking, such as selling off subsidiaries which do not fit the core of the business, or explain the company's strategy to analysts in such a way that the share price rises to reflect an accurate, rather than an undervalued, view of its stock. Once a bid is made, it is hard to do this, because any disposals or other capital restructuring have to be approved by shareholders.

When it is clear that a takeover bid is going to fail, what does the bidder do? There are occasions when a predator can come badly unstuck. Almost certainly he will have built up a parcel of shares in the company in which he is interested, although his bid will be conditional on sufficient acceptances to give him control. No one is expected to make an unconditional bid, but, once the fever is over, it can be difficult to recover the price paid for a block of shares on a rising market, and the bidder may be forced to take a loss. In such cases it is normal for him to arrange a placement through his brokers, in much the same way as when raising capital for his own concern. It is not unusual for the shares to be picked up by forces sympathetic to the company that has successfully defended itself against takeover, for the last thing directors want is an unstable market, especially if some of the allegations made in the heat of the moment seem likely to have stuck in the minds of the market.

A more interesting development occurs when an unsuccessful bidder actually walks away from the event with a large profit – an increasingly common event. Sometimes this can be achieved through barefaced cheek, especially if the subject of a bid has a group of directors and a large shareholder determined to hold on to their property at all costs.

This is what happened as a result of a visit on 20 November 1979 by the publisher Rupert Murdoch to his father's old office at the *Herald and Weekly Times* newspaper group in Melbourne, Australia, where he cheerfully greeted Sir Keith Macpherson, the chairman and chief executive, with the glad tidings that his News Group was about to present the Stock Exchange with the terms of a $A126m. bid for just over half of the company. Since the offer valued *Herald and Weekly Times*, the country's largest newspaper group, at $A100m. more than News Group, Macpherson suggested that the whole idea was ridiculous.

Perhaps it was; one newspaper later suggested it was like a snake trying to swallow a sheep, and similar metaphors were used when five years later, the entrepreneur, Robert Holmes à Court, made a bid for Australia's largest company,

BHP, and was described, colourfully, as 'trying to rape an elephant'. Murdoch, however, knew what he was up to. He wanted the *Herald and Weekly Times* desperately – ever since his father, whose genius had built up the paper, had died, he had set his sights on it – but he suspected that he would not get it, even though News Group offered $4 a share, a premium of $1.26 on the market price.

His suspicions were correct. His bid caused panic at the headquarters of another newspaper group 400 miles away in Sydney. John Fairfax Ltd, a conservative family concern, had a minority stake in *Herald and Weekly Times*, and its newspapers were bitter rivals of Murdoch's. Apart from the extra power Murdoch would gain if he controlled HWT, he would become a partner of Fairfax in two other major enterprises, Australian Newsprint Mills, the country's only newsprint manufacturer, and Australian Associated Press, the national news agency, both controlled jointly by Fairfax and HWT. Fairfax instructed its brokers to buy all the HWT shares it could muster to thwart Murdoch, and the prices rose quickly to well above the $4 that Murdoch had offered. Within two days Fairfax had laid out over $A50m. and had acquired 15 per cent of HWT. The shares stood at $5.52. Murdoch knew that he was beaten, but he saw a lucrative way out. Instead of conceding defeat, he instructed his brokers, J. B. Were and Co., to continue buying shares but on a much more limited scale. At the same time he commissioned another broker, May and Mellor, to unload the 3,500,000 shares he had already purchased. The Fairfax people, convinced that Murdoch was still a buyer, snapped up the lot, paying top prices, only to face the humiliation of hearing that they had been outwitted and that Murdoch had quit, using one of his own newspapers to condemn the Fairfax 'rescue' of HWT as 'two incompetent managements throwing themselves into each other's arms at the expense of their shareholders'. Maybe, but the real point was that Fairfax was determined to stop Murdoch at any price, and paid dearly for it – for when the shares settled back down at a lower price, it had lost over $20m., plus the interest on the $50m. laid out to acquire the stock.

The trick is that your opponent has to hate the idea of losing his beloved company so much that he will pay almost anything to keep it. It is not a ploy that is encouraged by some of the more conservative bodies in the City of London, but it is fair game, and the best defence, if you are sure that the predator does not have the nerve or the money to go ahead with a bid, is to call his bluff, let him face the test of the market, and then take large advertisements in the financial press to deliver a wounding riposte.

In most contested takeovers the issue of who wins is decided by institutional investors, as the major shareholders. In Britain they are not quite as fickle as in the United States, on which more later, but increasingly the institutions are under pressure to perform. Stanley Kalms, whose Dixons electronics group won control of the electrical goods retailer Currys in 1984, accurately reflected the current attitude. 'Companies can only expect loyalty when their shares are performing well, and the market has confidence in the management.'

The New Takeover Game

'Speculators may do no harm as bubbles on a steady stream of enterprise. But the position is serious when enterprise becomes the bubble on a whirlpool of speculation. When the capital development of a country becomes a by-product of the activities of a casino, the job is likely to be ill done', wrote John Maynard Keynes in 1936. 'What kind of society isn't structured on greed? The problem of social organisation is how to set up an arrangement under which greed will do the least harm', said Milton Friedman, in 1973.

Those who promote takeovers – or believe that there should be no restriction other than a prohibition on monopoly – argue their case by saying that shareholders benefit by the maximization of share values. They also suggest that business is made more efficient, and necessary rationalization brought about, because large and indolent managements are forced to promote change, in order to survive. Be that as it may, the real reason for the frenzy of takeover activity in Britain and elsewhere is the desire of large numbers of corporate raiders to get rich.

As is usually the case, the Americans are well ahead when

it comes to exploiting the possibilities available to the corporate raider. Indeed, so sophisticated have US financial markets become that individuals are able to use an array of new financial instruments to play the same old games. One game, called appropriately 'Copycat', is to study the moves of renowned raiders like T. Boone Pickens, and to emulate them. You will be 24 hours behind, of course, but those who have followed this course in a bull market have seldom fared badly. Nor is there any need to use much of your own money; you can buy a stock option for a fraction of the real cost, exercise the option when the price rises, and then sell out for a large capital gain.

It sounds like, and is, the stuff on which the 1929 Wall Street crash was founded, but in 1985 there were record numbers of Americans playing the share markets, and using sophisticated methods to do so. Scores of computer programs became available for individuals to analyse their portfolio performances, and to carry out 'what if?' analyses. Some programs are highly advanced, and can detect prices of related stocks that get out of step with each other. Armed with his personal computer, and a copy of *The Financial Times*, the personal investor found he was almost as well informed as many professional investment advisers. There was no need to accept the low returns offered by his neighbourhood bank, or savings institution. Why should he not get the kind of interest, or strike the kind of deals, organized by the big boys? He wanted to climb on to the gravy train.

In 1980 only 49 million shares changed hands daily on the New York Stock Exchange. By 1985 this had more than doubled to 108 million shares. In this period prices rose sharply.

Two-thirds of the rise is credited by analysts as being due to a feverish increase in takeover activity. In the takeover field only twelve transactions valued at more than $1bn. took place between US companies from 1969 to 1980. In 1985 alone, there were more than 30 such deals, and some in the $5bn. bracket. During 1985 companies in the United States were acquired, wholly or in part, at the rate of eleven a day, reshaping the landscape of US industry and worrying the politicians as to whether it was good or bad for the country and the voters. Timothy Wirth, a Democrat

Congressman, chaired a House of Representatives Committee, which seemed unsure. 'These mergers are having as profound an impact on the American economy as the advent of the great railroads, the airplane, and the telephone.'

The 1985 takeover trail also had a new style about it; it was no longer a question of the giants swallowing up the minnows, for many modest-sized companies found that they could deploy shock tactics to buy up corporations previously thought to be beyond their reach. This new phenomenon was heralded by one T. Boone Pickens, chairman of Mesa Petroleum, a small energy producer based in Amarillo, Texas. Pickens adopted the same logic pursued two decades earlier by the legendary City of London corporate raider, Jim Slater. Observing that the low price of oil had driven the price of many oil and gas companies below the value of their book assets, and that, broken up, they could be sold for much more, Pickens's company, Mesa Petroleum, made almost $US1m. in profits by driving up the stock prices of one oil company after another by threatening to buy them and strip them down. In order to keep Pickens out, the companies and their supporters bought the stock he had acquired at a higher price. Pickens's biggest coup was to bid for Gulf Oil when the stock had been trading at about $41 a share. Chevron came to the aid of the beleaguered Gulf board, and the two oil companies joined forces in history's biggest ever merger, worth $13.3bn. Pickens and friends were relieved of their holdings at around $80 a share, allowing them to walk away with a capital gain of $760m.

Much of this American activity was fuelled by borrowed money, in which the leveraged takeover has been a favourite technique. A corporate raider would take a modest position in a large company, wait a short while, and then offer to buy the entire stock by making a takeover bid. Where would the corporate raider's small company raise these billions of dollars from, you may well ask? Simple. He would approach a broker specializing in the art of raising junk bonds for worthwhile causes. In 1985 $27bn. worth of junk bonds were issued, and yet 15 years ago they did not exist, even as a concept. According to the investment bankers, Salomon Brothers, this trend led to some $78bn. of equity vanishing in 1984, while companies added $169bn. in debt, the widest yearly gap ever. The investment banking firm of Drexel Burnham Lambert is credited with devising the junk bonds, and has most of the business.

The bonds, issued by the corporate raider's company and thus increasing its debt, offer investors a very high rate of interest, but have to be fully subscribed only if the corporate raider is successful. And if he is successful he can afford to pay the junk bond-holders their high interest, because he will have the assets of his newly acquired company to play with. In other words, the strength of the to-be-acquired company's balance sheet is responsible for its own downfall. And if the corporate raider fails? Well, his activities on the stock exhanges will have led to a sharp rise in the targeted companies' share prices, so he will have a tidy capital gain, even after he had paid out a few millions for the fees of the broker raising the junk bonds.

T. Boone Pickens was the first to use junk bonds arranged by Drexel in a takeover attempt, when he bid for Gulf Oil. Now Drexel has spotters searching for companies that can be carved up and sold for more than their stock market values, and a list of corporate raiders who are open to targeting a useful prey. As indicated, Drexel does not actually raise the money to back up tender offers, but obtains commitments from institutional shareholders to buy the bonds if the tender offer is successful. For making these commitments, the institutions charge a fee, which may range from 0.35 to 0.70 per cent of the amount they pledge – in other words between $35,000 and $70,000 for a $10m. commitment. Brokers also take a high fee, but often this is on the basis of shared profits with the corporate raider.

An Australian Invades

The British public, even many British stockbrokers, viewed this activity in the United States with a kind of detached bemusement. City reaction was one of studied indifference; it could not happen here. But the City was awakened to leveraged takeovers in the autumn of 1985, when a relatively unknown Australian, John Elliot, came to London and bid £1.8bn. for Allied Lyons plc, a disco food and brewing conglomerate with a clutch of well-known brand names, including Skol lager, Double Diamond beer, Teachers whisky, Harveys Bristol Cream sherry, and Lyons Maid ice cream. Under the chairmanship first of Lord Showering, and then of Sir Derrick Holden-Brown, its record had been solid rather than impressive, and Elliott believed that he had the management skills and financial acumen to produce a better result for the shareholders.

Although his company, Elders-IXL, with interests in breweries, sheep farming, and financial services, was Australia's second largest industrial concern, it was only one quarter of the size of Allied Lyons. Indeed, Elders, with its powerful Carlton and United Breweries subsidiary, producers of the world-famous Fosters lager, was just the sort of company that Allied might have sought to gobble up itself had Australia's restrictive foreign investment laws made such a bid possible.

There were many in the City who welcomed Elliott's abrasive style, but there was deep concern as to the way the bid was mounted, for most of the funds were to come, not from Elders' own coffers, nor even from Australia, but from loans from a consortium of American banks. These banks, led by Citibank, were providing a facility of £1.23bn., two-thirds of the cost. The Government referred the bid to the Monopolies Commission, not for any reason to do with monopoly, but because of concern at the financing arrangements. Whether the Commission, with its slow and arcane procedures, is the right place for a major issue of public importance to be debated is highly questionable; certainly the Government's decision was unfair to Elliott, and was seen by many as the achievement of some sustained lobbying. For a Government which purports to believe in decisons being taken in the market, it is strange indeed that it is unwilling to allow the decision to be made in the proper place – by the votes of Allied Lyons' institutional shareholders. Elliott abandoned the bid, and bought instead the Courage brewery group from another takeover predator, Lord Hanson.

Battle in the Courts

Across the Atlantic other forces were at work in the leveraged takeover game which were beginning to cause grave disquiet, particularly for those who subscribe to the old-fashioned view that since a public company is owned by its shareholders it is reasonable to assume that their interests come uppermost. The truth, of course, is a little different.

By an odd quirk of fate, one of the victims in a case which was to become known as the 'poison pills' case was Lord Hanson. More than half of Hanson Trust's income comes from businesses in the United States, where Hanson's partner, Sir Gordon White, runs an identical operation. In August, 1985, Hanson and White identified a major American company as a suitable case for the Hanson treatment – the SCM Corporation, a solid if dreary conglomerate which manufactured outmoded typewriters, processed food, pigments and an assortment of other products. On 21 August, Hanson Trust offered $60 a share cash for SCM Corporation, valuing the company at $755m. well below its market capitalization. Robert Morton, an analyst with brokers De Zoete and Bevan, told me at the time that this was 'in the mould of Hanson acquisitions: SCM is exactly the kind of company he goes for, a company which has already undergone a great deal of rationalization and sorting out, which perhaps has not been fully realized by the shareholders'.

The SCM management was horrified. Here was this lord from England buying their company at rock-bottom value. By all the precedents, it was clear that, before they knew where they were, they would be looking for new jobs. Fortunately for them the board saw matters the same way, rejected the Hanson bid, and refused even to talk to Sir Gordon White, despite several invitations to do so. It hastily called in its financial advisers, the redoubtable New York firm of Goldman Sachs.

Curiously, however, it was not Goldman Sachs that came to the rescue of SCM's beleaguered management, but Wall Street's largest broking house, the New York financial conglomerate Merrill Lynch Pierce Venner Smith and Co. Merrill Lynch's capital markets division, headed by a young go-getter, Ken Miller, was hungry for new business, and skilful in organizing what has become known as leveraged management buyouts. Within a few days, Miller and his team had come up with a means whereby, at the stroke of a pen, Hanson could be thwarted, the SCM management could save their jobs, and Merrill Lynch would receive a large fee.

So it was that on 30 August, only nine days after Hanson's bid, a new company was announced – legally a partnership between the SCM Corporation's management and Merrill Lynch, but founded by the Prudential Assurance Company of America. It offered $70 a share – $10 more than Hanson – for 85 per cent of the SCM shares, and promised to buy the rest out of SCM profits at some future date, through the issue of junk bonds, which, it was hoped, would trade at about $70. A confidential Merrill Lynch paper described the deal as representing 'one of the most asset-rich LBO opportunities we have ever encountered'.

The wily Merrill Lynch team hoped that Lord Hanson would withdraw, but they took sensible steps to protect themselves, and their fees, if he did not. If Miller pulled this one off it would be the first time that a leveraged management buyout had been successful against a tender offer for cash. But there was a risk, so a clause was written into the contract providing for a $9m. fee should the bid be topped and the arrangements terminated, in addition to the basic fee of £1.5m. for fixing the deal in the first place.

Lord Hanson proved their fears justified. On 3 September, Hanson Trust increased its offer to $72 a share. Unlike the first offer, which valued SCM at a bargain basement price, this was a much more attractive offer for shareholders. For a start it was all in cash, with no waiting around for junk bonds and future profits which might or might not appear. For the SCM management, however, if presented the same problem, the prospect of the sack, made even more certain as a result of their tactics in signing up with Merrill Lynch, and handing over $9m. of the company's money in fees. Sir Gordon White did, however, hold out an olive branch. On 10 September, after several failed attempts by telephone to contact SCM's chairman or board, he sent them one further invitation: 'We believe it is in our mutual interests, including those of your stockholders, management and employees, that we should meet promptly'.

There was no reply, for, behind the scenes, Miller and his team had again been hard at work, advancing another, much more ruthless, way of frustrating Hanson's ambitions. Meanwhile the $9m. fee had already been placed in escrow. The new plan was to strip out of SCM Corporation its two most potentially profitable businesses, in the sure knowledge that the Englishman would either lose interest or be left with a crippled business.

This tactic has become known as the use of the 'poisoned pill', although a more appropriate metaphor might be that of a scorched earth policy. In this instance, the SCM management and Merrill Lynch increased their leveraged buyout offer to $74 a share, but subjected it to a new condition; if Hanson or any other party got more than a third of SCM shares, Merrill would have the right to purchase the two most thriving parts of the SCM Corporation – the pigments and processed food business – at knockdown prices. The business would then be run by the same SCM management. These two businesses were to become known as the Crown Jewels, for Merrill Lynch obtained the options for a total of $430m. against the SCM board's own valuation of $400m. for the pigments business and $90m. for the foods division. For organizing this neat new arrangement, Merrill Lynch took a retention fee of $6m., investment banking fees of $8m., and dealer-manager fees of $2.75m., in addition, of course, to the $11.5m. already paid.

The next morning Hanson Trust withdrew its $72 a share offer, and spent $200m. buying SCM shares on the New York market; within a few hours it had acquired 25 per cent of the company. But on 16 September Merrill Lynch acted again. With the Manufacturers Hanover Bank acting as agent, it put the shares of the crown jewel subsidiaries in escrow, and apparently beyond Hanson's reach. At this point the lawyers took over, with the action moving to the New York District Court in lower Manhattan. In the end Hanson Trust lost the case, but the verdict was reversed in the subsequent appeal.

Discussion in the United States has ranged over whether the law courts are really the place to decide such matters, as well as whether the frenzy of takeover activity wastes scarce investment capital, inhibits innovation, and forces managers to sacrifice long-term goals to the next quarterly profits sheet. Kathryn Rudie Harrigan, Professor of Strategic Management at the Columbia University Business School, talked to me about the increasingly common tendency for stock market takeovers to be decided in courts of law:

> It is just one more in a string of devices that managers and their investments bankers have come up with to avoid being taken over when they do not want to be.

Is this new trend likely to be damaging to shareholders? Professor Harrigan thinks perhaps not, in that values are often forced up by what is essentially a game:

> It is a game, and it is a game that is played with great ritual, and is being played in many, many companies these days. It is often cheaper to acquire something than it is to build it from the ground up.

But she does believe that business will suffer in the end:

> I think it is damaging to the long-term health of the business, because when you are so busy satisfying these short-term requests of the financial community, who are looking for instant gratification from their investment, you often cripple the long-term ability of the company to be able to reposition itself to remain competitive in a changing environment.

Professor Harrigan also believes that the concepts of poison pills and crown jewels could be exported to Britain, now that the Big Bang has revolutionized the way the Stock Exchange works:

> The two capital markets are becoming very similar in the way that people operate within them, and the kinds of expectations they have of the companies whose equities they hold. And more and more of the equities are held by institutional investors, who have this kind of short-term expectation, and they want to see this quick pay-off on their investment. I think the kind of behaviour we see here, with these leveraged buyouts, will undoubtedly be appearing also in your stockmarkets.

The Fed Acts and Britain Procrastinates

As takeover battles become more complex, it becomes increasingly likely that more and more lawyers will be drawn into the corporate financial area. There are, however, likely to be strict limits placed on the way acquisitions can be financed by debt. While the British Monopolies Commission deliberated privately on the issue – in the context of the Elders-IXL bid for Allied Lyons – the Federal Reserve Board in Washington decided to extend its long-standing margin requirements to take in corporations that are set up only as entities to sell debt and finance the purchase of shares.

The Wall Street crash of 1929, brilliantly chronicled by John Kenneth Galbraith in his book of the same name, was brought about by excessive share speculation paid for with borrowed money. If prices were going up by leaps and bounds, why not borrow? The trouble was that when everybody did it, it spelt ruin. To avoid repetition the Federal Reserve's regulations have long dictated that loans for share purchases cannot exceed 50 per cent of the value of the stock being bought. But the rules have not applied to bonds, and until 1986 there was nothing to prevent a shell company being forced to raise debt finance through junk bonds, to fund a leveraged takeover.

One example that alarmed the US authorities was the successful move by Pantry Pride, a relatively unknown supermarket chain in Florida, to take over Revlon for $1.8bn. Pantry Pride, with the help of Drexel Burnham, issued $700m. of junk bonds. It knew that the funds generated by its own operations would not be sufficient to meet its new debt service and dividend operations, but once it had acquired Revlon it was able to finance these obligations from the sale of a number of Revlon assets.

'Abuses by some banks and financiers are feeding a takeover frenzy that strikes at the economic well being of this country', one potential victim of a leveraged takeover wrote to Paul Volcker, chairman of the Federal Reserve. 'They are engaging in stock and bond and credit schemes reminiscent of those of the 1920s – but on a multi-billion dollar scale.' By extending the 50 per cent rule to shell companies, Volcker has not ruled out using such tactics. He has just made them less attractive – 50 per cent less attractive, in fact. For those that have the stamina to engage in it, it is still an attractive pastime, so long as you can stay ahead of the game.

Some American states have also passed legislation to impede unwanted heavily leveraged takeovers; New York State has legalized a set of delaying tactics to frustrate predators for up to five years. T. Boone Pickens is not impressed; 'That sort of thing will just further entrench entrenched management.'

What will happen in Britain is anybody's guess. As mentioned earlier, the Government's attitude towards takeovers is ad hoc, and an inexplicable and inconsistent muddle. The Department of Trade objected to an Australian owning a major brewery, but there were no questions asked when the Arab Al Fayed brothers took over Harrods and the House of Fraser through a heavily leveraged buyout. A Canadian was able to take over the ailing *Daily Telegraph* without question, while United Newspapers, which did not own any Fleet Street newspapers, endured a long wait while the Monopolies Commission secretly studied their proposed bid for the *Express* newspapers. Cabinet Ministers openly feuded over whether the country's only helicopter manufacturer should come under the influence of the American United Technologies Group, or a European consortium.

At the heart of the problem is the Whitehall passion for secrecy. If the Companies Act or the Banking Act needs to be amended to prohibit leveraged takeovers, that should be a matter for the House of Commons not the Monopolies Commission or the Office of Fair Trading. The Monopolies Commission should confine itself to recommending whether any proposed merger is likely to reduce competition, or damage the public interest; and since these issues are ones that ought to be openly discussed, its hearings should be in public. And in the end it is worth remembering that the judgement of the Stock Market is likely to be based on a sounder premise than that of any politician.

7 Selling the Family Silver

It is a Wednesday evening in the Conservative Club at West Houghton, an unpretentious Lancashire village in the drab industrial belt between Liverpool and Manchester. A group of women, two of them the wives of packers at a nearby baked-beans factory, are discussing the price of British Telecom shares. All have a small holding, following the Government's decision to sell off three billion shares in British Telecommunications plc to the public, in what had been the world's largest-ever share sale. The women agree that they plan to hold on to their shares, even though they could sell out at a tidy profit. And they have become addicted to share ownership. Since the British Telecom issue, three of them have bought other shares. Says one: 'I have bought Marks and Spencer, I bought Rank Organisation and sold them again, and I am buying Dobson Park, because I think that will benefit from the end of the miner's strike,' 'I watch the prices every morning in the *Daily Mail*', says another, 'and sometimes I keep a watch on them through the day on teletext.' None of them, nor their families, had ever had shares before. 'I did not really know how to go about it, I did not know a reputable stockbroker, or how to go about finding one, and I certainly did not know the bank would do it. It was a matter of ignorance, really.'

The experience of West Houghton confirms that the real lesson of the British Telecom float has been that a vein of popular capitalism exists to be tapped in Britain. Some stockbrokers argue that, even without privatization of great state monopolies at the initiative of the Government, new conditions had come about to make share ownership attractive to the individual. For the first time for over a quarter of a century, it was possible to generate a better return on capital invested in equities and other financial instruments than from that great middle-class – and heavily subsidized – bolthole, the family home. It was also true that some alleviation in death duties and other capital taxes had resulted in many couples in their late forties and early fifties inheriting a useful sum of money, which they chose to invest rather than spend on material possessions. When a City firm of stockbrokers conducted two investment seminars to canvass new business, one in London and the other in Preston, they obtained a significantly better response in the North.

Yet it is impossible to conceive that the new zest for share ownership, particularly among the working classes, would have come about had the British Telecom float, with its hype, touring road shows, television campaign and gimmicks like bonus shares and vouchers to help pay the phone bills, not taken place. Before the British Telecom bonanza, only about two million Britons, or just over 3 per cent of the population, owned shares. One year later that figure had increased to almost 8 per cent, still low as compared with the 25 per cent of Americans who individually own shares. By the time British Airways came up for sale, one in three adults in Britain were shareholders.

Britoil

If the flotation of British Telecom was regarded by most as an unqualified success, then, nine months later, there came a development that raised serious questions about the whole privatization issue. The Government decided to sell its remaining 49 per cent stake in Britoil, the state oil company.

Because its sale of the first half of Britoil in 1982 had been a flop, it took no chances and reserved only 15 per cent of the issue for the public, offloading most of the rest to delighted institutions, British and foreign. The Japanese and Swiss, in particular, could not believe their luck, for the Britoil offer was made at a give-away price. With sterling weakening the week before the issue, they lapped the stock up.

The public followed suit. Having been told by the newspapers ad nauseam what a wonderful investment opportunity was presented by Britoil, the issue was oversubscribed ten times. Those applying for between 200 and 1,100 shares were allocated 100; those seeking between 1,200 and 1,400 got 150; and those greedy or wealthy enough to seek more than 1,400 were allocated none at all. The decision to rule out the more enthusiastic private investors was all the more reprehensible, given that Japanese pension funds and many others who could not conceivably be said to represent the British national interest had been awarded tens of thousands of shares.

Lazards, the merchant bank awarded the plum of handling the sale, showed an acute lack of awareness of public feeling by describing the issue as a great success. Undoubtedly, for them and for the Government, it was. But, for small investors, it left a bitter taste in the mouth. 'We were conned', said a letterwriter to *The Financial Times*. 'What a fiasco', said another.

The small shareholders, the individuals, so assiduously solicited by Mrs Thatcher and her Cabinet, had been left with a pig in a poke. What real use were 100 partly-paid-up shares? Bought for £100, they had, after listing, a market value of about £120. Those who wanted to take a profit could not follow the Japanese life assurance institutions and sell out. The £20 paper profit turned out to be worthless once the minimum £15 commission and VAT had been paid. And when allowance had been made for the amounts paid on cheques submitted with application forms and held by those handling the sale for an unconscionable time, those selling would have made a loss. And investors deciding to hang on to the shares were left with a piffling long-term investment.

Other aspects of the Britoil sale left those who question City self-righteousness with a feeling of acute discomfort about the thin line that separates ramping a stock – pushing its value rather like a greengrocer trying to sell off tired cauliflowers – and genuine attempts to awaken public interest. As with British Telecom, those connected with the sale avoided going on television, or on record in the newspapers, to say that the shares were a good buy, and to give the reasons. They refused to give television or radio interviews on the grounds that to do so would be to break the law, a doubtful claim. In any event they employed double standards, through the Whitehall device of giving non-attributable briefings to compliant City journalists, many of whom wrote favourable articles about the prospects for the Britoil float.

It was always considered that the Britoil offer would be a difficult one, particularly with the world oil price shaky as a result of desperate price-cutting within OPEC. Britoil lacked the near-monopoly allure of Telecom or British Gas, and suffered the public relations disadvantage of having been established by a Labour Government, with its first board appointed by no less an ogre of the City than Tony Benn.

Lazard Brothers, acting on behalf of the Government, decided on a massive public relations campaign to get Britoil a better image, well in advance of the announcement of the time of the sale or the price. It placed a series of advertisements designed to lift public awareness of the company and its achievements. The advertisements were unrepentantly bullish. The shares had hovered at £1.87, well below the kind of price sought by the Government to offer an attractive investment. There was no mention in the advertisements about qualms over oil prices, or what the Lex column of *The Financial Times* called a 'twice-in-a-lifetime offer shareholders can do without'. 'With the oil Britoil produces in a day', said the banner headlines, 'you could fly three Concordes to the Moon.'

Along with the advertisements, the first of their kind produced by the company, a hand-picked coterie of leading financial journalists were invited, three or four at a time, to a series of private 'off-the-record' dinners at Britoil's sumptuous headquarters with Britoil's managing director, its exploration director, and, occasionally, its chairman, and a senior executive of Lazards. Guests, both journalists and analysts, found their hosts hospitable and also disarmingly frank. The media, it was suggested, and with some justification, had been excessively bearish about Britoil. They had not thoroughly inspected the figures. Even if the oil prices slumped further, and that was an 'if', Britoil would still be able to break even, right down to as low as an unthinkable $6 a barrel, although such a dismal prospect would undoubtedly lead to a retrenchment of exploration activity. Britoil had some of the best acreages offshore Britain, and was also exploring abroad, particularly America. In setting up Britoil, the hosts said, Tony Benn had not been stupid – 'he made bloody sure we got some of the best fields'.

Inevitably the dinners were followed by a series of unattributed articles in the press reflecting this more optimistic scenario, and just as inevitably, Britoil's share price rose, as the Government hoped it would. By now the bandwagon was rolling. Brokers wrote to their private clients warning them they should not miss out on the Britoil offer. Bank managers handed application forms to favoured customers. It was the hype of British Telecom all over again. It may well be argued that there is nothing wrong with any of this, that *caveat emptor* applies to buying shares from the Government as much as to anything else, and, after all, small shareholders have not actually lost money, while the Government has found some handy cash with which to help fund its deficits. It would not matter at all, but for two factors. The first is that the Stock Exchange publicly proclaims its abhorrence of share-pushers, and in the case of Britoil there was share-pushing. The second is that, although the Conservative Government has repeatedly proclaimed its desire to spread share ownership, it has, in every issue with which it is involved, put powerful City interests first.

British Gas

Even more hype went into the sale in December 1986 of over four billion shares in British Gas, with the introduction to the nation's television screens nightly of an ubiquituous but enigmatic character called Sid. Clever if unsubtle advertisements by the Young and Rubicam agency urged viewers to 'tell Sid' about the opportunities for the public to buy shares in British Gas. One even had a pigeon fancier releasing his bird and saying 'there y'are my darlin', just go and tell Sid'. Right to the end of the campaign, Sid was never to be spotted; in the very latest advertisement a near-demented potential shareholder was seen climbing a mountain peak and peering through the mist crying 'Sid' at a shape that turned out to be nothing more than a startled sheep.

The British public gratefully accepted the offer like lambs – and why not? As with British Telecom, the Government had priced British Gas attractively and with a forthcoming election in mind – those who sold quickly were rewarded with a capital gain in excess of 20 per cent, and those who held the stock could look forward to cheaper fuel bills with the prospect of gas vouchers in addition to normal dividends. For every 100 shares bought, investors received a voucher worth £10 payable over a two year period.

Although the campaign was much criticized by City editors and the smart set – some were even disingenuous enough to call it a failure – it generated five million shareholders, and was fair. Unlike a previous issue, by the Trustee Savings Bank, who after giving priority treatment to their customers selected other applicants by picking their names out of a hat, the British Gas float managers, N. M. Rothschild and Sons, not only made sure that gas customers received privileged treatment but also that all who sought shares received a reasonable allocation. This was achieved at the expense of overseas and British institutions, whose allotments were cut back.

Rothschilds also adopted a more intelligent approach towards public relations, making sure that questions about the issue and the operations of British Gas were discussed fully and intelligently answered. In this respect there was no hesitation in exposing the highly competent but irascible chairman of British Gas, Sir Denis Rooke, to 'on the record' media probing. Not only was this a total contrast to the less open approach adopted in other privatizations, but clearly was a move in the public interest. Would British Gas just be a boring public utility with low growth prospects, he was asked? 'I would much rather be that than an all-singing, all dancing-lot who do not actually perform', came the reply. 'We performed during nationalization, and we shall continue to perform; it will actually be a lot easier when we do not have all those civil servants hanging on our coat tails.'

Rooke, an engineer by training, developed a distaste for bureaucrats during the ten years he ran British Gas as a nationalized industry, but indicated that he regarded City folk as only a marginal improvement. 'I shall not lie awake at night worrying about my share price', he told me, 'the Stock Exchange is all about fashion, it is not about anything else. I shall be concentrating on the long-term health of the business'.

British Airways

Once British Gas was safely out of the way, the Government set about another major sale, that of British Airways. This was nowhere near as easy, for although BA occupied a dominant position in the domestic airline market, it was exposed to a degree of international competition, especially from deregulated American airlines on the North Atlantic. The sale of BA had also been postponed twice. The excuse given for the two postponements was a legal case brought by airline maverick Sir Freddie Laker alleging that BA had conspired with other transatlantic airlines to run him out of business. The case was eventually settled out of court. But there were other unstated reasons, the most important being that performance figures did not match up to the macho image conveyed by the Saatchi and Saatchi advertisements – as 'the world's favourite airline'. In the spring of 1986 the airline suffered badly from a downturn in tourism to Britain, while it also appeared its revenue might suffer as a result of a British effort to persuade the European Community countries to encourage more airline competition by outlawing a number of practices, including the specious system whereby major national carriers pool the revenue from flights between their respective capitals. But the British gave up the fight, and BA continues to run non-competitive services with airlines like Alitalia and Air France at some of the highest prices per mile in the world. By the time the airline came to be sold in February 1987, its performance had shown a marked improvement.

As it contemplated an election, the Government planned even more privatization – such as the sale of the nation's electricity industry, the water authorities, and parts of British Rail, British Steel and the National Coal Board.

The policy was not universally popular. The former Conservative Prime Minister, the late, Lord Stockton, likened it to 'selling off the family silver'. Labour pledged to renationalize British Telecom and British Gas. But by the end of 1986, it was clear that privatization was not confined to Britain, and that across the industrialized world the political winds were shifting towards policies that placed more reliance on market forces and a reduced role for the state.

In France M. Chirac's government planned to dispose of the state-owned banks, the Elf-Aquitaine oil group, and other nationalized concerns. The German government planned to return Volkswagen to private ownership, while the Japanese had massive sales under way – that of Nippon Telegraph and Telephone, Japan Airlines, and the loss-making Japan National Railway. Italy, the Netherlands and Spain had their national airlines up for sale. Amongst industralized countries only Australia and New Zealand stood aloof from the policy.

Such political considerations apart, what are the benefits of privatization, and how do they affect the new Stock Exchange? The government case is that the privatization programme will promote efficiency, stimulate competition, and encourage wider share ownership.

Wider share ownership

It will be several years before the full benefits of privatization become apparent, but it is already possible to see one important gain. Scarce capital resources are being used more effectively, so that ultimately the return on capital employed will increase. Of those corporations that were privatized in early programmes, most are trading more profitably. Amersham International, Cable and Wireless, Jaguar, and the National Freight Corporation have done spectacularly well. Only one privatized concern – Readheads, a division of British Shipbuilders, bought from the Government by the employees – has crashed. Readheads was given considerable ministerial blessing at the time of its privatization, but its voluntary liquidation was conducted more quietly.

It also seems as if the privatization programme has done something to stimulate wider share ownership. One million investors first tested the Stock Market when they invested in British Telecom, and by the time British Airways had been sold in 1987it was estimated that one in three adults owned shares.

It is not just the numbers that have changed. Shareholders

have become younger and more evenly spread by social class. According to an opinion poll conducted for the Trustee Savings Bank, in 1983, 27% of shareholders were aged 65 or over, and 40% were aged between 45 and 65. By early 1987 only 17% were over 65, and 35% were in thc younger bracket. The proportion of shareholders in the AB social class has also fallen over the same period – from 56% to 35%.

Efficiency

Claims of greater efficiency, except in the use of capital, are also difficult to judge. At present there is only anecdotal evidence. The waiting list for telephones is much shorter. But, from the public's viewpoint, it is the same old British Telecom, with a lack of enterprise and drive. Americans and Australians in London are astonished to find that there are no public telephones on Underground platforms or amenity phones in restaurants and department stores.

Complaints about British Telecom have also increased since privatization. The Office of Telecommunications, Oftel, receives more than 1,000 complaints from the public each month, nearly twice the number received by the old Post Office Users National Council, but it is unable to quantify the extent of breakdowns because it does not have access to BT figures. One gets the impression that Oftel has given up. A spot survey by *The Observer* of 200 pay phones in December 1985, one year after privatization, found that 26 per cent were out of order in Birmingham, 30 per cent in Glasgow, and 44 per cent in South London.

Getting British Telecom to attend to a faulty phone is a nightmare. For some reason BT's engineers seem incapable of making an appointment, or keeping one, if a householder tries to discover what time of day they might arrive to carry out the work. They also do not seem to have access to BT's much-publicized radio-paging service.

The Telecommunications Users Association, a body which appears to be more effective than Oftel, has estimated that four million calls a day – one in twenty – fail to connect properly or are inaudible. It has argued that BT's image as a business that uses satellites, fibre optics, and microchips is a myth, and that the first year of privatization 'has brought no discernible improvement to the general range of BT services'. It is certainly hard to find evidence for the Government's claim that BT has 'undergone a cultural revolution'.

The purpose of this book is not to debunk British Telecom, but it is certainly not proven that privatization has made it a more efficient, market-aware organization. It was – and remains – an unappealing monopoly.

More competition

It is very doubtful whether privatization has stimulated more competition. British Telecom and British Gas were state monopolies; they are now private monopolies.

The Government built into the privatization of both monopolies organizations to ensure that they did not abuse their power: Oftel in the case of British Telecom, and an Office of Gas Supply to act as a watchdog on British Gas. In the case of Ofgas, it has the power to ask the Monopolies Commission to extend or change the licence for British Gas, as well as being able to intervene in the setting of contracts for other companies to use the corporation's pipelines. The most worrying aspect of the impotence of both Oftel and Ofgas is that most of their activities will take place behind closed doors, reflecting the Government's passion for secrecy.

In the case of gas, the Government has come up with an extraordinary ploy to dictate prices; it will allow them to go up in line with the inflation index, plus any extra costs associated with North Sea gas supplies becoming tighter, less a percentage to take into account the degree by which Whitehall believes British Gas should have become more efficient. By contrast, in the United States, where privatized utilities are the norm, tariffs are designed to allow gas companies to achieve an accepted return on capital, usually about 12 per cent. The issue is then over what should be accepted as capital assets, and the public, in the form of politicians, pressure groups or individuals, may interrogate executives in public about the utilities' investments and other expenditure.

The British Gas formula for determining price increases has been publicly criticized by Dr Irwin M. Stelzer, an American expert on utility regulation, managing director of the

New York arm of Rothschilds, and an adviser to the Thatcher Government. He told *The Financial Times:*

> If it doesn't allow adequate profits to be made, then you will know because the company will be unable to raise capital, but if profits are good after a few years, how will you know if they are monopoly profits, or the result of efficiency? The interesting thing to me about the British approach to privatization is that no one thought through the regulatory consequences. The British fear of an excessively protracted, detailed regulatory system is leading them to a system in which the customer is essentially without recourse.

In its 1985 background briefing paper *Privatization in the United Kingdom* the Treasury hints at another reason for privatization, and, I am sure, the real one – the fact that the proceeds of asset sales are counted as negative public expenditure, enabling the Government to claim that it has been effective in controlling the Budget. The paper states:

> The effect of asset sales, reducing public expenditure just as the purchase of assets by the Government increases public expenditure, is incidental to the Government's main purpose, which is to increase efficiency and competition to the benefit of the whole economy.

If one believes that the Government's vision extends for much more than five years, then perhaps this is a true statement. But credibility in such matters as fiscal and financial targets has never been one of the Government's strong suits. One is left with the sharp suspicion that the true reason for the sale of prime assets at bargain prices, mostly to institutions, is to pave the way for tax cuts in advance of a difficult general election.

Even hard-nosed City institutions, not generally known for their criticism of Tory policies, have found the Thatcher-Lawson argument that asset sales were incidental to government finances unconvincing. Stockbrokers, Capel-Cure Myers stated in an analysis of what they called 'the privatization boom':

> The Government has made major tax cuts, particularly income tax cuts, a high priority. The expansion of the privatization programme has therefore certainly been conveniently timed. More importantly, even if one chooses not to doubt the Govern-

> ment's sincerity, and even if one accepts that privatization may have major supply-side benefits, it has to be accepted that these benefits may take several years to come through. By contrast, the proceeds from privatization have an immediate, if one-off, impact on Government finances.

Capel-Cure Myers stated that the Government had only been able to keep to its nominal targets for public expenditure and the public sector borrowing requirement by stepping up asset sales from £2,25bn. to £4.75bn. a year, thereby enabling it to contemplate tax cuts without blowing out its deficit.

Stock Market Indigestion?

It is not the purpose of this book to delve too deeply into the political issues of privatization. The real question for the new Stock Exchange is where all the money will come from to pay for these record-breaking sales of state assets? The question is all the more relevant, given the tempo of other asset sales of a non-government nature, such as Laura Ashley, Abbey Life, and Virgin. Can the stock market digest the exceptionally heavy demands upon British investors?

Clearly most at risk is the equity market, and there are some technical risks as well as fears of a shortage of capital, the most obvious being that the sheer bulk of privatization issues may push up the proportion of British equities in well-balanced institutional portfolios beyond the level that prudent institutions would wish. There is a technical solution; institutional investors might well decide to consider private monopolies in a different context from other large companies. Who will be the first to start a privatized monopolies unit trust? One Canadian group, Wood Gundy, has already launched a global privatization fund in the belief that the first state-owned operations to be sold are likely to be among the best.

Another technical risk is caused by the Government's decision to sell its assets off cheap and with the benefit of massive advertising campaigns. The British Telecom issue was heavily underpriced, and although otthers have carried much less attractive discounts, the Government will be careful to avoid overpricing an issue. The effect of this is to increase the interest both of first-time investors, and of those who had previously abandoned the Stock Exchange for 'safer' forms of investment. Assuming there is no dramatic slump in market values, interest in Stock Markets will be sustained, and the flow of cash into shares is likely to continue, to the detriment of other institutions like the building societies. Since the building societies are little more than High Street money shops, they may be expected to form closer alliances with the Stock Exchange by acting as agents for stockbrokers, thereby adding to the flow of funds into equities, at the expense of property. In other words, fears of a cash shortage on the Stock Exchange are exaggerated. According to Capel-Cure Myers:

> The BT bonanza promises to ensure a healthy appetite for future privatization issues from other buyers outside the UK institutional sector. Overseas buyers are thought to be particularly eager to participate in future major issues, although political considerations may lead the Government to limit their allocations. Nevertheless, the UK financial institutions, whose holdings now account for almost half the total British equity market, may be called upon to subscribe to no more than 40 per cent of the extra asset sales being launched by the Government.

The brokers also argued that tax cuts, fuelled by privatization, would boost economic growth and thereby enhance the general prospects for the equity market. This is debatable. There are those who believe that tax cuts will serve only to increase the nation's import bill, especially if sterling remains a relatively hard currency.

A boost to the economy will come from reduced gilt funding, however. With the public sector borrowing requirement lower than might otherwise be the case, the Government's gilts activities will not crowd out the other markets, and therefore interest rates could stabilize or even come down.

8 The Stock Exchange Grapevine

'Until the mid to late 1950s, modern investment analysis did not exist. Company research consisted of lunch with the chairman' – Gordon Pepper, senior partner, Greenwell & Co.

There has been an explosive growth in the financial information industry, which has increased the pool of knowledge about the Stock Exchange and the companies traded there to the point where it is now well beyond the capability of one person to digest it all. Gone are the days when a stockbroker would sit in his first class rail carriage from Sevenoaks to Charing Cross and comb through the pages of *The Financial Times*, working out his share tip of the day. Once at the office, he would telephone his friends and relations, and they would all be on to a good thing. A former City Editor of the *Daily Express* once told me that he had bought a house in the stockbroker belt and always travelled in a first-class compartment so as to be able to pick up such juicy tit-bits from those who were habitually on the same train. The journey home would usually be spent in the buffet-car where, over a beer or two or three, the successes of the day and the tips for tomorrow would be discussed.

In the late 1950s, the City Editor was a man of great authority, with an arrogance that could come only from having a considerable following of small investors. I remember Patrick Sergeant of the *Daily Mail* informing readers, just before leaving for his annual holiday one August, that they should not buy or sell any shares until after he got back. Patrick was not amused when he returned to find an anonymous telegram saying: 'Now that you are back, can we buy? – signed Pru and Pearl.'

City Editors also conducted their business with a certain panache. They would arrive in the office after a long lunch smelling of port and accompanied by a cloud of cigar smoke. Even today, several Fleet Street City Editors are provided with dining rooms, at which they entertain City luminaries and government economic ministers. One or two others have a regular table provided for them at the Savoy Grill.

But nowadays most media organizations, with the exception of the popular tabloids and BBC Television, which treats City stories with an almost total indifference, have an army of financial journalists reporting on the activities of the Stock Exchange. There are people who specialize in company news and comment, there are subject specialists on everything from energy and chemicals to banking and telecommunications. There are economics writers, and personal finance writers. who spend most of their working lives writing to fill the spaces left after the salesmen have filled their sections up with advertisements from unit trusts and building societies. Naturally they write mostly about unit trusts and building societies.

Then there are specialist publications, which include *Financial Adviser*, *Money*, *Money Management*, *Money Observer*, *The Investors' Chronicle* and *What Investment*. *Money Management* is especially useful for unit trust holders, because each month it analyses the track record of all unit trusts and insurance funds. There is also a wide range of tip sheets, promoted by aggressive advertising and persistent mailshots. Some are one-man operations; others are fathered by established organizations like *The Financial Times* whose Stockmarket Letter is marketed with uncharacteristic hype.

In the broadcast media there is a radio programme, 'Financial World Tonight', which has a thorough and reliable coverage of market activity and company news, and includes each night at least three interviews with company chairmen, stockbrokers and other active players in the market. Unfortunately, such is the present BBC management's lack of interest in business matters, that the 'Financial World Tonight' is not heard until 11.15pm. A weekly programme, 'Moneybox', has a large audience, and deals mainly with personal investment. On television there are two weekly magazine programmes, 'The Business Programme' on Channel Four and 'The Money Programme' on BBC2, both transmitted on Sunday evenings. Unfortunately both operate only for seven months of the year, and there is nothing that concentrates specifically on the Stock Market, like 'Wall Street Week' and 'Moneyworld' in the United States, where there is also an excellent programme, 'Nightly Business Report', on PBS, as well as an all-day, five-days a week 'Financial News Network' on cable. So, in the United Kingdom at least, investors have to turn to the press for information, with *The Financial Times* offering the most comprehensive coverage, although recently it has come under stiff challenge from the European edition of the *Wall Street Journal*.

But if the press has made great strides in the last decade in the spread and depth of its financial coverage, it is no longer the only, or even the major, source of information. The real explosive growth in the financial information industry has come from stockbrokers themselves, with almost all the major broking houses running their own publishing operations. These brokers are not only using the computerized printing technology that Fleet Street unions have managed to keep out of their news rooms and composing rooms, but also pride themselves on being able to get their publications out fast. On Budget day, for instance, some broking firms, as well as a few firms of accountants, will have their analysis of the Chancellor's measures in the hands of important clients before the newspapers.

Brokers' publications fall into two categories. There are regular weeklies or monthlies which contain a detailed review of the major economies and their financial markets, and offer a number of recommendations. Their forecasts have a high reputation for accuracy, usually better than the Treasury's. Amongst the regulars are Phillips and Drew's monthly outlook, which is always good reading. There are regular specialist publications also, such as Grieveson Grant's *Japan Report* and *US Report*, Salomon Brothers' *Financial Futures*, and *Options Analysis*, Yamachi's *Investment Report*, and Vickers da Costa's *International Investment Outlook*, and Drexel Burnham Lambert's *International Investment Monthly*, which is an excellent 35-pager. Then there are sector or subject reports, which look at either a company or an industry in great detail, and come up with recommendations.

Investor Relations Managers

The rise of the specialist broking press has been such that the financial directors of large companies, and their public relations men, often spend more time wooing brokers' analysts than talking to financial journalists. A new corporate breed has emerged, the investor relations manager, whose job it is to keep both institutional investors and analysts informed of the favourable aspects of thh company. They now have their own body, the Investor Relations Society. Many of its members have lavish expense accounts, and jet in and out of two or more European capitals a day, expending great energy and charm on their subjects. Things can, however, go wrong. I remember the investor relations executive at Olivetti wringing his hands at an unfavourable broker's circular on his company written by a very presentable woman analyst, and crooning down the phone: 'How can you do this kind of thing to me?'

In recent years increasing attention has been paid by the major European companies to soliciting investment in the United States, and those who have neglected this aspect of financial public relations have done so at their cost. Had Unilever, for instance, been prepared to take a stronger public profile in the United States, the outcome of its important takeover bid for Richardsons-Vick might have been different, and the company might not have fallen to arch-rival Proctor and Gamble. Before, during, and after the bid, the Unilever board declined to talk to either *Forbes* or *Fortune* magazine, nor did they take the opportunity of appearing before the New York Society of Security Analysts daily lunch, which is now televised and distributed by satellite to over 360 leading portfolio managers and almost 1,000 of the nation's top analysts by the Private Satellite Network.

A contrast is provided by ICI, which maintain a full-time investor relations executive in New York to keep analysts at both institutions and broking firms up to date with the company's financial affairs. Some of the information is printed material, but another aspect of the job is to organize an annual road show to five American cities. There are also quarterly meetings allowing all major US analysts to meet the company's finance director and other top members of staff, and visits are arranged for those who wish to tour ICI's operations in Britain.

Investor relations specialists are now having to deal with an extra medium – specialist television. In the summer of 1985 PSN, a company headed by William Miller, a former Treasury Secretary and chairman of the Federal Reserve Board, and backed by major Wall Street finance houses, launched the Institutional Research Network (IRN), a private television network for the professional investment community. Each day, publicly traded corporations, investment bankers and research brokers provide financial programming to the analysts, portfolio managers and investment officers of the institutional investment firms that shape world financial markets.

The subscribers to IRN, which include such major institutions as Fidelity, Aetna, and Prudential, controlling in total $800bn. in assets, receive a 21-inch colour monitor, a videotape recorder, and a decoder. From its control centre in New York, IRN remotely turns on and off the recorders and electronic programme guide printers, so there is no need for anyone to man sets until they wish to view.

The network has already been used by major corporations for a variety of planned and last-minute presentations, such as takeover battles, discussion of quarterly earnings, new product announcements, new management introductions, and chief executive interviews. Merrill Lynch has used the network to link Sheraton ballrooms across America so that invited interested investors could question their top portfolio investment experts in New York. It now also has a regular half-hour weekly programme on IRN at close of business on Wednesday, usually bringing in house experts to discuss particular topics, such as tax reform or growth stocks.

It remains to be seen when such a network will be operational in London. When I canvassed such a possibility in the City, the caution of the financial establishment emerged. 'I cannot imagine brokers wanting to watch television in the office', said a partner in a major firm, forgetting of course, that many of his staff do little but stare at screens containing information. 'I do not think the City would want to go in for this kind of show business', said another, again totally missing the point. He had just come from lunch at the

Butchers' Hall at which Pirelli's president had made a long presentation, using slides and other visuals which were indecipherable, and at which questions had to be cut short for lack of time. Most of the analysts present complained, not about the cooking, which was excellent, but about the quality of information available. Had they been able to see the Pirelli chairman, American style, in a well assembled but no-frills television production, they would have learned more.

City conservatism is not the only problem, however. After all, many companies, such as British Telecom, Commercial Union, Westland, the Trustee Savings Bank, and Coopers and Lybrand have learned of the benefits of using taped television for communications. But without the speed and cheapness of satellite and cable, a City network cannot be firmly established. Unfortunately the Government allowed the BBC and IBA to procrastinate for so long over the development of satellite television that private networks have not yet been started.

The Analysts

The profession of stockmarket analyst is one of the greatest growth areas in the City. Once the analyst was the office introvert, who spent his day hidden from view in a corner behind a pile of dusty papers, fretting over obscure charts while his broking colleagues got on with the business of trading shares.

Securities analysts have now formed an industry in their own right, and have their own professional body. It is a highly competitive business, and one in which the rewards can be considerable. There are even annual contests for best analysts and broking firms, sector by sector. The best known survey, now the Extel Ranking of UK Investment Analysts, was started in 1973 by Continental Illinois, and is based on a detailed questionnaire sent to investment managers of the major institutions. Only four out of ten bother to reply in detail, but this still makes over 90, with £240bn. of funds in their care, and the survey is self-perpetuating, as the winners can count on many a new job offer and a stream of telephone calls from journalists, merchant bankers, accountants and others also anxious to tap their expertise.

In 1986, the survey decided that the top research brokers were James Capel, Phillips and Drew, and Scrimgeour Vickers, out of 161 firms that featured in the results. Surprisingly, perhaps, the top trio were exactly the same as the year before. What was different was that investment managers polled showed a marked trend away from the selection of particular individual analysts towards the recognition of entire teams, probably a reflection of the increased numbers in many sectors and the firms' own reluctance to rely on individuals who might be hired away. Extel Financial's survey showed that one in ten of the top ranked analysts had changed jobs during the year.

The survey also indicated how specialist analysts have become. The typical analysts covers no more than two sectors, and analyses 34 companies. Their average age is 33, and the typical analyst will have spent only three years with his or her firm. Analysts, while widely quoted by the media, are by no means universally loved. As the fruits of their endeavours seem to be more widely disseminated, with some members of the trade now regular television pundits, a number of companies have turned against them. In early 1987, GKN announced it would be attending no more analysts' lunches, and would not permit its executives to speak to them except on well-orchestrated presentations twice a year. The company apparently prefers to deal with fund managers direct. Its their choice, of course, but one cannot help feeling that this provides yet another example of British management being reluctant to face facts and to present themselves more forcibly.

The job of an analyst is part office-based, part on the road. He or she – and there are an increasing number of women in the business – has access to high technology, particularly numerous computer programs designed to make the postulation of future trends easier. An analyst will also spend a lot of time on the telephone asking questions, as well as attending briefings and seminars. In recent years it has become customary for companies, particularly large companies, to make life as comfortable as possible for analysts, transporting them en bloc or individually to expensive country hotels, where it is possible for them to socialize with directors and senior management as well as to talk shop. A thorough briefing of analysts just before a company's results are published can be crucial in getting a good press, for increasingly newspapers are dependent on the views of analysts for comment. Expectations can be lowered, if profits are going to be bad, and vice versa. Some companies choose an exceptionally attractive venue for six-monthly or yearly meetings with analysts; Olivetti's Carlo de Benedetti, for instance, favours Florence, where the men and women from broking houses across Europe can sample art and Tuscan wine as they endeavour to digest the problems of the Ivrea company's 'marriage' with the American giant A T and T. Pre-privatization, British Airways flew opinion-makers in the City to a variety of overseas locations in the old but not mistaken belief that the further away from home the closer the mind might be concentrated on the subject in hand.

Often oiling the wheels that make the information industry function is the City public relations firm. Financial public relations companies like to think that they are a cut above their contemporaries in the West End who deal with products and services, and they probably are. Their senior people certainly behave better, and have larger expense accounts. Their role is also much more important. There are legal obligations on companies who make financial changes to inform the press, and someone has to ensure that announcements are hand-delivered round the City at the right time, usually in late afternoon. There can be no question of sending out details of an acquisition, or a rights issue, on an embargoed basis.

But City PR advisers are no mere messenger boys. In many cases they are the eyes and ears of a company chairman and, occasionally, his voice. Some company chairmen are gregarious and well-connected individuals, able both to project a positive image and to be sensitive to public opinions. The majority are not. A good PR person will be able to keep the chairman and directors informed of shareholders' opinion, what the newspapers are saying and, increasingly important, an assessment of political and Whitehall opinion. If needed, he will be able to lobby politicians on the company's behalf. In major takeover activity, or in rights issues, the public relations man will also become a valuable aide to merchant bankers and stockbrokers.

If those groups already discussed form the fabric of the financial information industry, who provides the basics? Both in this country and overseas these are in surprisingly few hands. As soon as a bargain is struck, or an announcement is made to the Stock Exchange, it is picked up by reporters of the Exchange Telegraph company, better known as Extel, and instantly circulated on ticker tape and video monitors. Within seconds of a sale being made, a financial intermediary in his office one mile or 10,000 miles away may look at his video screen and see the price, pick up the telephone, and call a broker.

The prices of international stocks are carried on the Reuters Monitor, an international network which has more than 50,000 terminals connected to it, and provides business, corporate and international news as well as prices on almost anything that is traded.

The Stock Exchange has its own in-house computer network, called Topic, which is being heavily marketed and carries the price information available on SEAQ, the off-the-floor trading system that replaced dealing through jobbers on 27 October 1986. Apart from detailed prices, Topic carries company news and Stock Exchange announcements.

Then there is a Telerate, in which the US Dow Jones Company, publisher of the *Wall Street Journal*, has a major stake. With 14,000 subscribers, each paying an average of $700 a month, Telerate provides a constant barrage of financial information. Its 'Page Five', an electronic summary of US bond and money market prices updated every minute, is compulsory viewing in Wall Street.

For those who just want to keep abreast of events – and major price movements – without going to any serious expense, Prestel offers a batch of services. Or simpler still, you can use Ceefax and Oracle's price service on the ordinary television set.

Finally many stockbrokers themselves have electronic information services of a high order. Scrimgeour Kemp-Gee has 'The Ticker', similar in concept to Page Five on Telerate, which monitors the top 900 British shares, and displays the 30 most recent price changes on the screen, rises in red and falls in blue. Another page gives US prices. Datastream, pioneered by Hoare Govett, and now owned by Dun and Bradstreet, provides detailed graphs and charts, many of which are used in *The Financial Times*.

Financial Advisers

With such a wealth of information available, to whom does today's investor turn for advice, and from whom can he obtain the most reliable advice? It is an easy question, and it is perhaps the one that is most frequently asked by those with more than a few pounds to invest. It is also one of the hardest questions to answer.

One quite correct answer is no-one. In the end the investor, whether the chief investment manager of a large insurance company or a widow in Worthing, has to make the decision as to which is the best vehicle for improving the value of his or her savings. It is possible, even for those who do not consider themselves financially literate, to have cheap access to a great deal of information, and even that is sometimes of less use than a hunch or an everyday observation. For instance, anyone who has watched the development of Britain's High Streets over the past ten years will have noted the rise of Marks and Spencer. Shopping at Marks is not cheap, but its goods are of high quality, and its stores are full. Goods are seldom discounted, not even when adjoining stores are holding cut-price sales. Anyone reading the details of the M and S credit card, and its very high interest rate, and reading in the press of the large number of cardholders, will see that profits from this source will grow. You may not make a quick profit on M and S shares, but they will grow, along with British Telecom, British Airways, and smaller concerns like Trust House Forte.

But this is to dodge the real question. To whom can one turn? A bank manager, stockbroker, accountant, building society manager, perhaps. All have their place and purpose, but none of them is a good investment adviser. Today's bank managers are notoriously poor; they tend to shy away from giving direct advice, steering customers in the direction of in-house unit trusts, which with few exceptions, have not been the best performers. They do not seem to know much about the Stock Market, which perhaps explains why, in the average bank, the day's copy of *The Financial Times* is often out in the waiting room and not on the manager's desk. Accountants are useful tax advisers, and usually save you the cost of their fee, but when one talks investment to them, they start talking about complicated accountant-run pension schemes for the self-employed, and property trusts. Building Society managers live or die by the balances on deposit in their branches, so it is not easy to accept their views as impartial. This leaves stockbrokers, who can be either good advisers or bad advisers, but mostly are a mixture of both at the same time.

It has been my experience, and that of almost everyone I know, that a stockbroker is all smiles when first approached and when he is about to get your account, but thereafter the service deteriorates rapidly. Occasionally a broker will advise you to buy, but seldom does he seem to advise you to sell, unless you have given him discretion over your account, when he appears to be buying and selling without rhyme or reason, a process, which if taken to extremes, is known as 'churning'. Half the time the problem is never knowing whom to ring at the brokers' office, because the names, and voices at the end of the line, change all the time. One broker, Hoare Govett, has tried to solve this kind of problem with its new Dealercall system, whereby clients are given a plastic card with a number; they quote it when phoning and are then automatically put through to their dealer. The minimum transaction, however, is £750.

In the United States things are a bit different. Stockbrokers take their business to the public, and in almost every prosperous suburb there will be one or more open-plan broking offices, laid out rather like a large travel or estate agents, where the public may call, enjoy a cup of coffee, and discuss their investments with a consultant. There is plenty of literature available, including both brochures and financial magazines, the *Financial News Network* and Wall Street prices run continuously on television monitors, and there is a friendly unpressured atmosphere. It is a pity that the only equivalent meeting place in Britain's High Streets appear to be the betting shop; to all but those with substantial business to transact, stockbrokers' offices are forbidding places. In the United States, it is also now possible to discuss your finances in the money shops that form an important, and profitable, part of Main Street.

The changes in the City arising from the Big Bang, particularly the mergers between stockbrokers, banks and other financial institutions, will lead, I am sure to concerted efforts being made to make their financial advisers more easily approachable. It will also lead to the growth of another branch of the financial services industry – the independent financial adviser, the person who is not employed by a bank or broker, nor is rewarded by a handsome commission from a unit trust management company or a life assurance company, but who charges for his services on a time basis, in the same way as an accountant, architect or solicitor. Growth of such an independent sector is, however, likely to be slow, for the British do not like paying for services which they feel are theirs, by right, for nothing.

9 Towards a Clean Stock Exchange

'I am a regulator, a watchdog, and a policeman, in that order' – Sir Kenneth Berrill, chairman of the Securities and Investments Board.

'Regulators cannot eliminate risk. Profits and risk run together. Investment – as distinct from saving with a bank or building society – necessarily entails taking deliberately considered risks. The aim is to see risk taking fairly rewarded, to foster the spirit of enterprise, but to reduce the scope of losses resulting from fraud or concealment of risk' – White Paper on Investor Protection, January 1985.

At four o'clock in the morning of 23 October 1812, three men called at the Popincourt Barracks in Paris with the devastating news that the Emperor Napoleon had died beneath the walls of Moscow. It was a plausible story – news from the campaign front took three weeks to get back and the French armies had just achieved a great victory at the Battle of Borodino that had opened the gates to the Russian capital. The men also said that the Senate had abolished the Empire and appointed a Provisional Government, and was calling on the 10th Cohort of the National Guard for support. Within hours a huge conspiracy against Napoleon was under way, and the Emperor's leading supporters were thrown into prison. That story, told in more recent times by Italian author Guido Artom, in his book *Napoleon is Dead in Russia*, was the inspiration for one of Britain's most notorious examples of share market rigging. In the early nineteenth century only major news moved the fledgling Stock Market, and it took headlines like 'Napoleon set to Invade', or, better still, 'Napoleon Dead' to move the market.

Since even then, in the days before the telegraph, old news was no news, stockbrokers often placed faithful retainers in the port of Dover to listen to the rumour mill, watch the sea, talk to fishermen, and report back regularly. And so, when, on 21 February 1814, Colonel de Burgh, alias Charles Random de Bérenger, turned up in Dover in a red uniform, saying he was aide de camp to General Lord Cathcart, and reporting the death of Napoleon and the fall of Paris, the news flashed to London at the speed of a pony and trap. Although foreign reporting was severely limited in those days, along with share ownership, there were those in London who had heard of the earlier, unsuccessful, conspiracy against Napoleon, and the subsequent execution not only of the plotters but also of the soldiers who unwittingly carried the message. They were therefore very much on their guard against such embellishments. But 'Colonel du Burgh' had an elaborate story, a detailed account of how Napoleon had been butchered by the Cossacks. He had also made a point of going directly to the headquarters of the Port Admiral in Dover to appraise him of the facts. Surely, said brokers, it must be true.

Prices on the Stock Exchange shot up, as the wealthy clients of brokers received the news, apparently confirmed by hand bills distributed in the streets of London. They were not to know that these had also been handed out by de Bérenger who had himself taken a coach to the capital, to collect his gains, estimated at about £10,000. It was, of course, all pure fraud, but note that those who lost out were those who had been contacted by brokers, those who, themselves, were privileged possessors of inside information, which, in this case, turned out to be false.

Not much has changed in 175 years, for it is still those who are 'in the know' that stand to make rich pickings from speculative trading on the Stock Exchange. Latter-day frauds on similar lines to that perpetrated by de Bérenger were common in the early 1970s, during the so-called Australian mining boom. Reports of a nickel 'strike' by an obscure and barely known and usually recently listed mining company would reach Sydney as a result of a tip from Kalgoorlie, a remote dusty gold town in Western Australia. Confirmation was impossible, but the word flashed round, and the price of the stock shot up. I worked for a financial magazine at the time, and the Financial Editor would return from lunch, very excited, and shout something like 'Bosom's Creek has struck nickel', and rush to the phone to buy shares. Some brokers made a point of reserving shares for journalists, who could be counted upon to write favourably about a mining prospect, which, more often than not, when the geologists' reports arrived, turned out to be nothing more than a hole in the ground or a stick marking a spot in the desert. Fortunes were made and lost, and the secretary to a prominent Australian politician made over £100,000 from share trading in Poseidon.

Each day, as soon as the London Stock Exchange opened there was feverish activity as investors sought to cash in. Many had their fingers badly burned, and the two year 'boom' earned Australian brokers a bad reputation which they have only recently lived down. As one merchant banker, who frequently visits Sydney, put it: 'The Aussies saw it as a way of getting their own back on the Poms'.

Ramping stocks was not confined to those on the fringe of share markets. Writing in *The Observer* on 5 September 1971, under the headline 'Digging up the Dirt', I reported how an Australian Senate Committee investigation into the series of mining collapses and false claims in that country had severely shaken investors' confidence.

One thoroughly dishonest practice disclosed to the Committee was the purchase of huge blocks of shares in early trading by certain brokers, using their house accounts. By lunchtime, word would be round the markets that a particular share was on the move, and the broking house would unload its newly acquired holding at a substantial profit. Those shares that remained unsold would be allocated to clients for whom the firm held discretionary accounts, at a substantially higher price than the firm had paid for them, thereby enabling it to take a profit at its clients' expense. To add insult to injury, the clients would be charged brokerage, but usually would be none the wiser, for they would see from the *Australian Financial Review* that they had apparently obtained the shares at the 'market price'.

The Committee's report makes interesting reading, even 15 years after the inquiry. It scrutinized in detail the accounts of one sharebroking firm that had gone into liquidation, only to find that about 80 per cent of the firm's trading was on its own account, and that its income from commission amounted to only a minor proportion of turnover.

Another prominent Sydney stockbroker, who was also a director of two major mining companies, was exposed for trying to have one of the companies taken over by a joint venture operation, in which his stockbroking firm's affiliated investment house had a stake. Evidence to the Senate Committee revealed that the stockbroker planned the takeover without informing the company chairman or his fellow directors, and that an associate company of his firm was to act as the underwriters.

Let us move back to London, and to 13 June 1985. It was a typical summer Thursday on the Stock Exchange. Trading was languid, as is so often the case at this time of the year. Then came a sudden burst of activity, much to the curiosity of the party from a Norfolk Women's Institute that was visiting the public gallery that day. Someone was buying large blocks of shares in Arthur Bell and Sons plc, and their prices rose by 14 per cent.

The visitors had to wait until reading their Saturday edition of the *Eastern Daily Press* to find out why. Guinness plc had made a bid for Bell on Friday the 14th, and on the eve of that takeover offer, someone had got wind of what was going on, and had been buying Bell's shares furiously in the hope of a quick profit. Like most people who cash in on a 'hot tip', the miscreants were never discovered. Yet 'insider trading' is strictly forbidden both by the law, which since 1980 has made it a criminal offence, and by the rules of the Stock Exchange. Despite that, as a practice, it is rife.

According to Philip Healey, editor of the magazine *Acquisitions Monthly*, the share prices of takeover targets have risen on average by between 20 and 30 per cent in the month before a bid. Over 90 per cent of prices move before a bid. One reason for this may well be that astute investors have spotted, from their own research, likely targets for takeover; after all, you did not need to be a genius to forecast that once the Imperial Group had rid itself of its Howard Johnson network in the United States, it would be an attractive target.

But, that apart, the Stock Exchange says that in each recent year it logged more than 2,000 suspicious price movements a month, and referred some of the worst cases to the Department of Trade and Industry.

The Stock Exchange maintains a special squad of men and women at its Throgmorton Street offices to try and track down insider traders. That means questioning those suspected of using inside knowledge to make money, and putting the evidence before the Exchange's Disciplinary Committee.

New and powerful computers allow them to spot erratic price movements both in London and on other major international markets, and they have the authority to question anyone who works for a member of the Stock Exchange, which, since 'Big Bang', includes a large number of international banks and other financial conglomerates, but not, as yet, legal and accounting firms. Their computers have instant access to all Stock Exchange transactions over the previous six months, and they may manipulate the data base by asking over 100 questions. On November 4 1986 their data base turned up the deal that led to the downfall of Geoffrey Collier, who resigned from the prominent merchant bank, Morgan Grenfell.

But just like detectives from the regular police forces, they rely more on hot tips from informants than from the craftsmanship of a Sherlock Holmes. Since 'Big Bang' the number of tips has been increasing to more than ten a week. Many of them come from market makers in the City using the SEAQ terminals, and spotting something suspicious. Since the new system means that market makers can lose thousands of pounds by incorrect pricing, they are very aware of phoney figures.

They also have the backing of compliance officers employed in securities houses – a relatively new development. These men and women make sure that both the Stock Exchange rules and their own house rules on share trading are strictly observed, and if they spot an irregularity in a transaction involving another firm usually report it to their opposite number.

Some companies are stricter than others in the code of conduct they insist staff must obey when buying and selling stock in their own account. Chase Securities insists that all transactions are placed through the company, and that compliance staff are notified. At Barclays de Zoete Wedd the phone transactions of all dealing staff are logged, so that investigators could, if they wished, find out who telephoned whom and when. Some firms plan to take this a stage further – and tape record all phone calls.

Even so, many insider traders escape detection. One particular problem is the use of nominee companies in offshore tax havens as the trading vehicle. The head of the squad, Mike Feltham, and his team of former policemen, computer consultants, stockbrokers and accountants, say they often follow good leads only to come up against a brick wall when a block of shares is purchased by a nominee company. 'There is no way we can see at the moment of busting offshore companies without international cooperation', Feltham told me. 'All the old names are always there – the Cayman Isles and so on. But it is not only in the Caribbean or in Liberia that this problem exists – much closer to home in the Channel Isles or the Isle of Man we have just no hope of getting behind the nominee thing.'

'Another big problem is that when we want to interview someone who has dealt in the market, we have absolutely no power to go and talk to that person unless he or his firm is a member of the Exchange. In America, for instance, it is very different. An investigator can get a subpoena more or less immediately.'

The Department of Trade and Industry

Although the Stock Exchange is doing its best to prevent insider trading and other forms of dishonesty it is not the principal policeman of the City. That role belongs to the Department of Trade and Industry, a bureacracy whose responsibilities range from promoting Britain's export effort to monitoring and allocating regional development aid.

Until the passage of the Financial Services Act, the DTI was almost totally ineffective in policing City crime. Between 1980, when insider trading became a criminal act, and 1986, the Stock Exchange sent it the results of more than 300 rigorous inquiries, with a third of them containing strong evidence of culpability. But only five cases went to court.

In many ways the DTI was less effective than the Stock Exchange, which at least had the power to discipline errant members. As one civil servant told me:

> The Department of Trade and Industry has to work through a much more rigid legal framework. We have to meet the stringent requirements of the Director of Public Prosecutions, and therefore have to obtain a very substantial burden of proof, which is not always easy.

That is not the only problem. The Department has not been helped by the low morale of the whole of the Civil Service and matters are made worse by the high turnover of senior adminstrators. Also, in the three years to 1985, the ministerial team has been changed twice, and there have been five different Secretaries of State.

There is also the worry that Whitehall and Westminster are remote from the City action. Number One, Victoria Street, is a different world from Throgmorton Street. Most of the staff of the DTI have no outside commercial experience, and the Civil Service promotion system is not geared to the development of expertise. In order to regulate the City, there is a need for specialists in the law and practice of companies, competition and investment, and in accountancy, but in the relevant part of the Companies Legislation Division there was, until recently, no post for a qualified lawyer or chartered accountant, and of the 47 officials working in this area, only four were in the division at the beginning of 1980. Under the present government controls, the DTI has been unable to increase pay or promotion prospects to the level needed to attract good people.

The US Securities and Exchange Commission

The problems of organizing a prosecution, coupled with the inadequacies in the way the DTI has operated, led many to argue that Britain should establish a powerful regulatory body, based in the City, and staffed by professionals, in the mould of the US Securities and Exchange Commission. The SEC, with a staff of 1,800, was established in July 1935 following the Wall Street crash of 1929. A Congressional investigation found that there had been stock manipulation on a huge scale, blatant dishonesty and insider trading, and the SEC was established with sweeping powers over the securities industry.

All corporations have to file quarterly financial returns, and much more detailed annual ones, with the SEC, as well as reporting to it promptly any facts or important events which might affect the market for the company's stock. Federal laws require companies planning to raise money by selling their own securities to file with the Commission true facts about their operations. The Commission has power to prevent or punish fraud in the sale of securities, and is authorized to regulate stock exchanges. The law under which it operates lays down precise boundaries within which directors, officers and large shareholders may deal in the stock of their companies.

In its time the SEC has notched up some notable successes in prosecuting corporate crime. In August 1968, it filed charges of securities fraud against 14 Merrill Lynch officers and employees. In the end Merrill Lynch publicly consented to an SEC finding that it had used advanced inside information from the Douglas Aircraft Company for the advantage of preferred institutional clients, defrauding the investing public of an estimated \$4.5m. in the process – no mean sum at the time. Unlike the British Department of Trade and Industry, the Securities and Exchange Commission is a mecca for bright young lawyers who wish to make their name as determined investigators, and then, as often as not, get out into lucrative private practice with the SEC name on their credentials. Just after the SEC netted Dennis Levine, a senior executive of Drexel Burnham Lambert, for insider trading, in the spring of 1986, I flew to New York to look at how the organization worked. Was it really more efficient than the self-regulation the City favoured? One was immediately struck by the professional approach of the organization, and the determination of its officers to pin down the crooks. There was nothing amateur about it, like the British system whereby a Government minister, with other things on his mind, appoints 'inspectors' who again have other things to worry about, and other jobs to go back to once an investigation is finished. 'We will go to the end of the earth to pin these people down', one SEC official told me proudly. 'Our only obstacle is that some countries are not cooperative. But increasingly that is changing.'

The SEC has much wider powers than the Department of Trade, and has much more inclination to use them. The DTI so far has been reluctant to use its power to force open bank accounts and to demand documents, though that may change. But the SEC may subpoena individuals and companies in the US, and demand sight of their bank accounts. Outside America it has agreements with the British, Japanese, Swiss, Cayman Isles and other governments to gather information, and it can also call for sanctions to be imposed on the US branches of non-cooperative foreign banks. Offenders may not only be prosecuted, with penalties as high as three times the illicit profits, but the SEC will turn over all the evidence it has gained to civil litigants who have been disadvantaged as a result of someone's insider trading.

Even these powers are inadequate when one considers this definition of the modus operandi of an insider trading provided by the *Financial Times:*

> The would-be insider trader gets a job with the corporate finance department of a merchant bank active in mergers and acquisitions. Always travelling via a third country, he visits two tax havens, Panama and Liechtenstein, which have resisted foreign pressure on their secrecy laws. In each company he sets up a trading company, and opens bank accounts in two or three banks in their names. He only uses banks with no operations or assets in Britain or the United States. He never tells the banks his real name, but arranges for them to deal through a large London broking firm whenever they receive coded instructions over the telephone.
>
> When he picks up inside information, he always trades alone using a call box. He never trades in large amounts, but may break up a transaction into a series of deals from different accounts. He avoids the mistake of trading just before a bid announcement – it makes the market makers vengeful.

As the *Financial Times* pointed out, the SEC's achievements 'highlight the passivity of the DTI'.

Curiously, though, it was the SEC's biggest coup, catching Ivan F. Boesky, the self-styled 'king of the arbs', that provided the DTI with some of their best leads into City fraud this side of the Atlantic.

Boesky was brought to book because of the Levine case mentioned earlier. Levine pleaded guilty, paid back $12.6m. in illegal profits, and sang like a canary to the SEC, implicating Boesky. Boesky was charged with making a personal killing on insider information provided by Levine, fined $100m. dollars, barred for life from working on Wall Street, and ordered to dismantle his $2bn. firm.

Boesky was one of the biggest and best known speculators in the feverish takeover business in America, using a phenomenal network of contacts to make huge profits through arbitraging. Like Levine, he also 'cooperated with the authorities', which is a euphemism for becoming a supergrass in order to keep out of jail.

His testimony, including taped telephone calls and recordings of meetings, opened up a Pandora's box of illicit insider trading across the world, particularly in London, which has always pretended that the City was cleaner than elsewhere as a result of the famed 'Word is My Bond' maxim and similar 'holier than thou' expressions.

It was soon apparent that nothing could be further from the truth. Within days of the Boesky revelation, the Trade and Industry Minister, Paul Channon, introduced stiffer rules. Soon after some of the DTI's own officials were the subject of inquiry, while a major investigation led by a Queen's Counsel and an accountant was launched into the role of Guinness and the Morgan Grenfell merchant bank in the former's takeover of Distillers. Boesky had been a large shareholder in Distillers during the bid.

In early 1987 the murk of scandal shrouded the City. Everyone said more big names would be revealed as insider traders. The Government, facing re-election, feared a major scandal, but avoided the professional approach and the establishment of an SEC. It continued to put its faith in amateurs, through self-regulation.

The British Compromise

It was not that the Government lacked evidence on the need for better policing of the stockmarkets and other City activity. As far back as 1981 the Commissioner of Police of the City of London had produced a report, largely ignored at the time, which said that fraud had got out of hand.

> Events of the year have demonstrated that a problem which has been in the background for some time is now fully to the fore. It stems from the inadequacy of legislation which exists for the purpose of protecting depositors and of controlling the activities of companies in the business of handling funds on behalf of the investing public. The Acts have sought to control by registration, and their failure arises from inadequacies in the procedures for vetting applications, and from the lack of requirement for any controlling authority to exercise supervision over the trading of companies whose registration has been accepted. They are ineffective because they cannot control the dishonest companies whose activities they were intended to curtail.
>
> The result is that the Fraud Squad has been called upon to investigate the failure of investment companies whose financial difficulties could have been observed at a much earlier stage by a competent authority making standard supervisory checks, for example an examination of audited accounts. The problem is likely to remain with us until legislation, regulation and control is made more effective.

In 1981 City fraud had risen by 42 per cent, and it has risen ever since. Clearly self-regulation was not working. In the course of his inquiry Professor Gower himself came up with an apposite summary of the problems faced by the Stock Exchange and other bodies in enforcing self-regulation:

> On the old boy net, they are likely to have their suspicions aroused earlier, and they can undertake less formal investigations more rapidly. In recent years, if these investigations revealed possible breaches of legal rules, they have shown a commendable willingness to pass on the information to the Department of Trade.

Unfortunately, by now, the villains would have a fair idea of what evidence was being marshalled against them, and would be either busily briefing their lawyers, or planning a one-way trip to a warm country with no extradition treaty with Britain. As Professor Gower put it:

> Even if there is a strong case, the more serious the offence the less likelihood of a conviction there may be. Long delays will probably be incurred before the prosecution can be launched and heard, and unless there is a 'guilty' plea, the trail may take

> weeks or even months, and a jury is likely to be baffled by the complicated evidence. The costs may be enormous. Hence there will be a temptation to press lesser charges to which the defendant is willing to plead guilty.

And, in a passage on Stock Exchange self-regulation, he said:

> When the breach is of their own regulations, one of their main difficulties is that of enforcing observance of regulations by those who are not members of the agency. This can be avoided to some extent if the agency affords facilities to non-members, and makes those facilities conditional on agreement to comply when listing companies – as the Stock Exchange does when listing companies. Even so, its ultimate sanction – a suspension of the listing – is a somewhat ham-handed one since its principal victims are the probably innocent shareholders, and not the guilty management.
>
> As regards enforcement against their own members, their powers are effective so long as those members wish to remain members of the agency and value their repute in the eyes of their fellow members. If they do not, even the sanction of expulsion is ineffective.
>
> A major advantage which the self-regulatory agencies enjoy is that those hearing a case may be better able to appreciate the significance of what may appear to others to be a technical breach. The corollary, however, is that they may seem to be concerned to protect their own, and to ignore the public interest.

So why not have an American-type SEC, with the power to mount swift public investigations? Professor Gower found that 'criticism in City circles of the SEC as a mammoth, lawyer-dominated, over-regulatory bureacracy is greatly exaggerated', but nevertheless he shrank from recommending the establishment of 'anything so elaborate'. Undoubtedly he was swayed by the old maxim that 'politics is the art of the possible', for he declared:

> such a recommendation would clearly not be accepted by the present Government which dislikes quangos. While it would have influential supporters among the Labour Party, it too has always failed to establish a Securities Commission when in power – under less unfavourable economic conditions than at present. I do not imagine that the Liberal-SDP Alliance would be any more enthusiastic about facing a head-on collision with the City establishment. For I have been left in no doubt of the City's rooted objection to a Commission.

Professor Gower also pointed out that the American example was seen as part of the Roosevelt New Deal, and thereby attracted to its staff some of the most able and idealistic products of the universities and law schools. A British body in the 1980s would not, he felt, have similar appeal. And in recommending the course that the Government was later to adopt – the delegation of new and tougher regulations to bodies like the Stock Exchange – Professor Gower unearthed a quotation from one of the founding fathers of the US SEC indicating his belief in the ideal of having a self-regulatory organization:

> so organized and so imbued with the public interest that it would be possible and even desirable to entrust to them a great deal of the actual regulation and enforcement within their own field, leaving the Government free to pursue a supervisory or residual role.

Gower added, wryly:

> In the United States that ideal was not achieved, partly because in 1938 it was dramatically revealed that the leading self-regulatory agency, the New York Stock Exchange, could not then be regarded as sufficiently 'imbued with the public interest'.

The Financial Services Act

When it acted, just before Christmas 1985, the Government compromised, with a classis Whitehall fudge. Essentially the City would be left to police itself, through the creation of a number of self-regulatory agencies, one of which is the Stock Exchange. But to keep them on track a Securities and Investment Board has been created, staffed by professionals and headed by Sir Kenneth Berrill, a former head of the Central Policy Review Staff, now abolished, which will be empowered to carry out a large number of tasks delegated to it by the Department of Trade and Industry. The Department, however, retains the right to be the final arbiter. Almost all of this regulation and policing of the investment industry is to take place in secret, as is increasingly the tendency in Britain.

The mainspring of the Financial Services Act was to bring

all the 15,000 investment businesses in Britain under the aegis of a recognized licensing system. The definition of an investment business runs to three pages in the Act, and includes all stockbrokers, financial advisers, bond, futures and money market dealers as well as scores of those in the field as sales staff, marketing everything from unit trusts to endowment policies. The term 'investments' covers:

i) Stocks and shares in British or foreign companies.
ii) Debentures, including debenture stock, loan stock, bonds and certificates of deposit.
iii) Government and other public securities including gilt-edged stock, local authority bonds and bonds issued by foreign governments and international organizations.
iv) Warrants entitling the holder to subscribe for shares or bonds.
v) Depository receipts for shares, bonds or warrants.
vi) Units in collective investment schemes including units in unit trust schemes and shares in open-ended investment companies.
vii) Options on currency and on any other investment.
viii) Futures contracts for commodities.
ix) Contracts for differences whose value is linked to the value of any kind of property, or to an index – for example the Stock Market index.
x) Insurance policies which are investments, such as endowment and unit-linked policies, but not pure term assurance or policies which simply protect against risk.

To operate in any of these fields without a licence is illegal, and the law extends to those giving advice and managing investments as well as those actually dealing or arranging deals. So the days when anyone could open up an office in the High Street and call themselves an investment adviser are gone.

It is a criminal offence to make a false or misleading statement as a sales pitch, and those trying to sell shares, unit trusts or any other type of investment are supposed to declare what they are getting out of it by way of commission or otherwise. They are also bound to give the client advice according to his needs: thus, if you are a pensioner with a capital sum seeking high income at low risk in order to provide yourself with a regular income, investment advisers will be committing a crime if, for instance, they try and push you into cocoa futures.

Trust accounts

The Act also provides long overdue protection for trust accounts. If you buy a house you will normally be asked to pay a 10 per cent deposit upon signing the contract. Until you complete the transaction, that money is normally held by the estate agent effecting the sale in a trust account; that is, the agent cannot use this money for his day to day operations. The same applies when a solicitor has funds in trust. In each case the customer is protected by law from default by the estate agent or solicitor.

Until now the same protection has not applied to investors. If an investor has in his possession a share certificate, he is protected. But if money is entrusted to dealers, brokers or management companies for investment, the client has little protection; his money and investments may not have been segregated from the firm's money and investments. It is one thing to lose money because an investment adviser or manager makes an unwise decision; that is part of the risk of using a professional investment adviser, for there is no guarantee that fortunes are to be made. But it is another for the client to lose money because it has disappeared down a bolthole along with the investment management company.

The Government realized that, with fixed commissions at an end and intense competition for business, it was inevitable that some broking houses, investment management companies, advisers or quasi-advisers would go bust. If investors' funds were being maintained in what firms euphemistically like to call clients' accounts – and not in proper trust accounts – the hapless saver would never see his money again.

Those who have dealt with members of the Stock Exchange have been well protected. If a member firm fails, its assets and those of all its partners immediately belong to the official Assignee, who may make an ex gratia payment from the Stock Exchange Fund established for this purpose. The Financial Services Act now protects everyone, for money held on trust will have to be kept in a separate account from a firm's own money, and cannot be lent out to the firm or to another client. There have in the past been relatively few fund managers who have absconded with savings entrusted to them, but plenty of examples where they have proved incompetent. Now they cannot use money in a trust account without full written authorization.

Life assurance and unit trusts

Other groups brought within the Act are life assurance and unit trust salesmen, some of whom have earned an unsavoury reputation for preying on the elderly and the unsophisticated investors.

The direct sales force of life assurance companies may number several thousand. As a group, they are almost invariably self-employed, which weakens the control the company can exercise over the individual salesman, and contributes to his insecurity. Members are recruited largely from those without relevant prior experience or qualifications. They are usually given a two-day course, and then sent out to build up a local clientele under the loose supervision of an area manager. Newspaper advertisements sometimes state that they may expect to earn up to £30,000 per annum. That is technically possible, after time, but most will be lucky in the first year if they earn £6,000. They are rewarded mainly by commission, though they may receive a modest contribution towards their own office expenses. Most of the work is by cold calling. One method is to scan small advertisements – particularly births, deaths, marriages and engagements – and then follow up the family with the suggestion that the time is appropriate for a discussion on financial planning. If a salesman signs up a client, the client may cancel within a ten-day cooling-off period. The companies have argued that their training courses stress the need for ethical practices and that their salesmen face dismissal if they breach the company's code of conduct. But accounts by those who have been on some of these courses suggest otherwise. The warning that you won't get in if you say you are selling insurance seems often to be stressed. One salesman's opening gambit is 'I have been asked by the Government to explain to people the advantage of insurance-linked investment'. Others say they are conducting public opinion polls.

Then there are industrial life policies, where premiums are collected weekly or monthly by a salesman calling door to door. Sometimes the amount collected is only a few pounds. Most of the salesmen are employees of their companies, and are also trained to give advice about other types of insurance. Industrial assurance is subject to additional legislation which provides for the business to be supervised by the Industrial Assurance Commissioner and the Chief Registrar of Friendly Societies, who acts as an Ombudsman and arbitrator in disputes between them and their industrial policy-holders.

New coldcalling rules

Unit trusts have been marketed in the same way as life assurance, though under tougher rules. Under the Licensed Dealers (Conduct of Business) Rules, a dealer has not been able to deal in securities during, or as a result of, a call in person or by telephone, unless the call was at the client's express request.

The new law has cracked down on cold calling for both life assurance and unit trust selling, in fact the Financial Services Act has banned it altogether, with only two exceptions. Calls on professional investors are permitted, and canvass calls will also be permitted where the salesman offers a contract with a cancellation clause within a 'cooling-off' period. Even where permitted, the call will have to be undertaken in accordance with strict ethical standards, which will require early identification of the caller and purpose of the call, will seek to avoid the call being a nuisance to the person called upon, and will ban altogether selling under the guise of market research, which is a common phenomenon.

The majority of life assurance companies have welcomed the new rules, but the members of the Linked Life Assurance Group, who sell unit trusts linked to life policies often as a means of supplying personal pensions, are bitterly opposed. They wanted a rule whereby intermediates would have only to disclose commissions that departed from a standard industry scale, but the SIB wisely would have none of this, and insisted on the full commission that is being paid being revealed to the client. Almost everyone else in business lets those who pay for a service know how much it will cost them, so why not those that sell unit trusts, even if the true revelations come as something of a shock to clients?

Most people think that insurance brokers are above all this, and that when they approach an insurance broker they can get fair, sensible, honest and independent advice. They may be lucky, but it must be remembered that insurance brokers are subject to the same inducements in favour of particular types of policy as direct salesmen, and that the broker is rewarded by commission in exactly the same way.

The notion that brokers choose the best option for their clients from a very large range of companies and underwriters is mistaken, except perhaps in the case of the very largest firms. Professor Gower stated in his report:

> This is because insurance companies like to establish a connection with a known list of brokers, and brokers find it convenient to establish a connection with a restricted list of companies. In addition to paying brokers straight commissions on each transaction, some companies pay them overriding commissions based on the total volume of business they bring to the company, thereby providing a powerful inducement to channel business to a restricted number of companies. Companies have been known to offer brokers interest-free loans to help finance their businesses. The mutually understood implication is that the loans will not be recalled so long as the brokers place most of their business with the lending insurance company, but will be recalled if they do not.

All this has now changed with the Financial Services Act, and brokers are obliged to offer a 'best option' and a reasonable choice for clients, and to disclose to them the nature of their arrangements with insurance companies. They will also have to register with a self-regulatory organization (see below).

Faith in Self-Regulation

As explained earlier, the Securities and Investments Board will exercise most of the comprehensive statutory powers delegated to it through a number of autonomous self-regulatory organizations, of which the most important will be the Stock Exchange and the National Association of Securities

Dealers and Investment Managers (NASDIM), a body which includes firms dealing and broking in securities and collective investment products as well as investment managers and advisers. Other groups likely to be working as similar self-regulatory bodies are the International Securities Regulatory Organization, which includes firms dealing and broking in international securities, international money market instruments, forward agreements, and related futures and options; the Association of Futures Brokers and dealers, whose firms work in futures and options markets as well as conducting investment management and advice; the Investment Management Regulatory Organization, which covers investment managers and advisers; the Life Assurance and Unit Trust Regulatory Organization, which handles life companies and unit trust managers; and the Life and Unit Trust Intermediaries Regulatory Organization, whose members are brokers. As can be seen, some of these bodies overlap, and by the time the new regime is in operation in late 1986, there may be some changes.

These bodies will be the ones that licence investment businesses, although it is possible for the SIB to license individuals who do not wish to join any of the self-regulatory organizations. Those applying for authorization directly will have to show they are 'fit and proper persons', by providing a business profile, and details of their financial strength.

The new rule book

Also planned is a comprehensive rule book, drafted by the SIB, which was, in early 1987, still being studied by the DTI, long after the Financial Services Act had received the royal assent. One of the most important rules will be what I call the 'smoking is harmful to health' warning, similar to that carried on cigarette packets. This will apply to all investment advertising. In future, what the SIB calls 'simple but clear risk warnings' must be included in all advertising matter, which includes newspaper and magazine advertisements, television, radio and video promotion, and leaflets. According to the SIB:

> These statements, will draw attention to three types of risk: the volatility of a particular investment – for example that shares

may fall in price as well as rise; the liquidity of the investment – for example that a long-term insurance contract may not be encashed at an early stage without some early loss, or that stocks in which there is no organized market may be difficult to sell at a fair price; and finally potential future liabilities, for example the obligation to pay a variation margin on a futures contract.

Advertisements will also have to be fair, accurate and complete. The severity of the application of these principles will vary according to the form of advertisement – the simplest requirements being for advertisements which carry little or no message, and the most stringent for advertisements asking readers to post a cut-out coupon with money. In the case of the latter, the rules will require fair and complete disclosure of relevant facts, and the substantiation of all statements of fact.

Also planned is a 'Know Your Customer Rule'. In recommending the purchase, sale, exchange or retention of any investment, a firm would be required to have reasonable grounds for believing that the recommendation is suitable, having regard to any facts known to it as to the customer's financial position. Similar requirements will apply to a person acting as a discretionary manager on behalf of a client. The Board will require firms to take reasonable steps to obtain from customers who are not professional investors the information necessary to make this judgement.

An important new rule being drafted is one to prevent the practice known as 'churning', whereby those running discretionary portfolios of shares and unit trusts for private clients, buy and sell them indiscriminately in order to pocket the commissions or other profits available to the firm. This practice is extremely difficult to prove, and safeguards are not easy to devise. Beyond a general prohibition on excessive transactions, the SIB is planning to require regular reporting to the client of the firm's earnings on his account. Another general rule will relate to excessive charging of clients.

Chinese walls

The Government has stamped fairly firmly on a novel ploy canvassed by the Stock Exchange and others in financial markets to prevent insider trading and corruption – the establishment of 'Chinese walls' between the various branches of a company.

Any of the new financial conglomerates has the power simultaneously to act as banker to a company, raise long-term debt or equity, make a market in the securities involved, retail them to investors, and buy them as managers of discretionary funds. The object is to establish a barrier of silence and confidentiality between those carrying out these tasks, so that they do not enjoy advantages not shared by competitors, or the investing public.

The theory of Chinese Walls is that John Smith, involved either in raising funds for a company or organizing a disposal, will not seek to influence Peter Brown, in the fund management department, either by seeking his support in a purchase, or tipping him off about a possible sale. It is a good theory, dependent 100 per cent on the integrity of everyone involved, but it is inconsistent with all the standards imposed on those who face conflicts of interest in other areas of commerce, politics and local government. One definition of the practice runs as follows:

> A Chinese Wall is an established arrangement whereby information known to a person in one part of the business is not available, directly or indirectly, to those involved in another part of a business, and it is accepted that in each of the parts of the business so divided decisions will be taken without reference to any interest which any other such part or any person in such part of the business may have in the matter.

To help physically to create Chinese Walls, some companies have actually separated functions into different City buildings, often half a mile apart. For example, Hill Samuel and Co Ltd, merchant bankers, occupy offices in Wood Street, just opposite the headquarters of the City Fraud Squad to the south of the Barbican development, while Hill Samuel Investment Management is on the north side of the Barbican, in Beech Street. Lazards operate their own Chinese Walls within narrower confines. Overlooking a drab concrete square on Moorfield Highwalk is Lazard Brothers and Co Ltd, the merchant bank. Thirty yards away, on the adjacent side of the square, and separated only by a pedestrian walkway, is Lazard Securities Ltd, the fund management arm of the company. Equidistant from both is a large and well-patronized wine bar and hostelry, the 'City Boot' – exactly where the Chinese Wall is supposed to be. Both at lunchtime and in the early evening it is packed with Lazards' men, not the clerks and typists, but the middle-rank officers of both companies. It strains credibility to imagine they do not talk shop.

Wisely the Government decided that, even though most reputable financial groups can be trusted, it had to do more to protect investors from conflict of interest. The White Paper of January 1985 put it simply enough: 'Chinese walls of silence between different sections of a firm cannot be relied upon'. Sir Martin Jacomb, deputy-chairman of Barclays Bank, agreed. 'Chinese walls are only effective if their foundation is the self-interest of the investment bank creating them. In other cases there is unlikely to be much public confidence in them'. Professor Gower added this observation:

> City opinion has been remarkably complacent about this, apparently believing that reputable firms can be trusted to resolve the conflicts in such a way that if anyone suffers it will be they and not their clients. That will not be so, however, unless they invariably ask themselves the vital question: 'Would we mind disclosing to all concerned exactly what we are doing?' And if the answer is yes, not doing it without full disclosure and the consent of those to whom it is disclosed. Unhappily, as recent events have shown, they do not always ask themselves this question or, when they do, always draw the right conclusion and act upon it. This is one of the reasons why no section of the investment industry, however great its prestige, can be excluded from the regulatory system, and why all must be under an enforceable obligation to disclose. Conflicts of interest or duty cannot be avoided. But failure to disclose can, if all are subject to rules of disclosure which are effectively monitored and enforced.

So the new SIB is making rules requiring a firm to disclose to the customer, both verbally and later in writing, the nature and relevance of any conflict of interest. If a client asks it to buy or sell shares in the XYZ company, and the firm is working as an adviser or underwriter for the company, it must say so.

Implementation

The SIB rules should make the City a much safer place for investors. By their very existence they will place a constraint on a number of unfair and undesirable practices. The small investor – the person buying unit trusts or small blocks of shares – will be the major beneficiary.

The trouble may prove to be implementing the rules. As has been clearly shown with another major City institution, Lloyds, strict rules are of little use when there is weak management and weak enforcement. Under Sir Kenneth Berrill, the SIB will be anxious to prove quickly that it is not a toothless tiger, but at the same time its activities seem to have been pushed into the background by the revival of activity in the Department of Trade and Industry.

Protecting the Euromarkets

Then there is the question of regulating the Eurobond market. Most buying and selling of Eurobonds takes place by telephone or electronic mail, and not in the Stock Exchange, and about 95 per cent of deals are cleared through two organizations, Euro-Clear Clearance Systems Ltd owned by Morgan Guarantee and Cedel SA, a French company owned by a consortium of banks.

In this case reputation is jealously guarded by an international professional association, the Association of International Bond Dealers, based in Zurich, where the Swiss Government has accorded it the status of a recognized legal entity. It has a full-time Secretary-General and support staff, and has established its own set of self-regulatory committees. In the event of fraud, forgery, or any other criminal activity, as well as breach of professional ethics, the AIBD can suspend or expel a member, who would then be shunned by professional market-makers. At present most Eurobond investments are held by institutional investors, as we saw earlier. But there will be an increasing trend towards such investments by small savers, either through funds of funds and unit trusts, or directly. After all, why should not the individual benefit from a blue-chip investment in a sound

Eurobond? It may prove to be much better than a building society. London branches of big American broking firms have already indicated they intend to offer Eurobonds to private clients. Inevitably the wider the spread of Eurobond investments – and the more people that get into the selling act – the more the need for the same kind of regulation as is being enforced on equity markets. Those who buy Eurobonds in Britain through a recognized investment exchange will receive the full umbrella of protection offered by the Financial Services Act.

Criticism

At the beginning of this chapter Sir Kenneth Berrill was quoted as saying that he felt he was a regulator first, a watchdog second, and a policeman last. And this, indeed, seems to be the major, and perhaps the only, real weakness of the new order.

When one looks carefully at the way the Financial Services Act will be policed, one is drawn back inexorably to the same problems: an understaffed, inexperienced, inadequate, department in Whitehall, and a regulatory network much given to the preservation of the status quo rather than to the exposure of City sharp practice. That being so, the system seems unlikely to survive the first major scandal, particularly when so many supporters of the Conservative Government are unconvinced.

One of the most influential sceptics, Sir John Nott, one-time Secretary of State for Defence in the Thatcher Government and now chairman of Lazard Brothers, the merchant bank, believes that it 'will founder politically in the next bear market'. Sir John has an interesting argument, believing that those in the Tory Party who are the most vocal against establishing a statutory body to regulate the City will be the first to demand one when things turn sour. He told a City symposium:

> When firms go bust, Parliament will cry foul. When firms bearing excessive overheads and taking new risks in the new environment go into liquidation and lose depositors' or small shareholders' money, a wholly statutory system will be irresistible. This will

> be the best protection also for the City because the small depositor and the widow will be perceived to have the full protection of statute based on the rule of law instead of the perceived protection of expert practitioners who will be truly exposed to parliamentary rhetoric and abuse. I do not like the prospect of City experts being parliamentary scapegoats for failures of the system.

Another problem with the plurality of self-regulatory bodies is that the standards are unlikely to be consistent. How can they be? Barclays Bank's Sir Martin Jacomb, first deputy chairman of the SIB, admitted that it will fail in its objectives 'if one self-regulatory organization becomes more attractive than another because its standards are lower'.

There lies the problem. It is relatively easy for politicians to legislate for investor protection, but Government has to make arrangements also to enforce the law. Yet, as we heard earlier, the relevant Ministries, such as the Department of Trade and Industry, lack adequate resources, while other units, such as the City of London Police's Fraud Squad, are woefully undermanned. The senior member of the Squad has said, perhaps inadvisedly, that so short was he of resources that frauds involving less than £20m. were unlikely to be investigated.

The position is no better at the department of the Director of Public Prosecutions, where a much-hyped Fraud Investigation Unit was set up in January 1985 to coordinate efforts on major fraud cases. One year later the Solicitor-General, Sir Patrick Mayhew, under questioning in Parliament, was forced to admit that its resources were 'seriously stretched'.

John Wood, the Deputy Director of Prosecutions, listed some of the other problems in a refreshingly frank interview with *The Financial Times:*

> I do not think we are justified in prosecuting where we think a criminal offence has been committed, but where the chances of conviction are pretty remote. These cases are extremely expensive. There is not a great deal of mileage in spending a six figure sum of money in the knowledge that the end result will be an acquittal.

Another difficulty concerns the mode of fraud trials, which have to be before a jury, and often last for months. British witnesses can, of course, be sub-poenaed, and forced to wait around for days on end to give evidence, but overseas witnesses are reluctant to agree to such inconvenience. Moves are afoot to move away from jury trials, and to admit sworn statements as evidence in the manner of the American system, but until the system is changed the trial of fraud cases will remain unsatisfactory.

John Wood said the DPP found the institutions cooperative, but not individuals:

> You have to remember that a witness in this country is not obliged to make a statement. If he does not wish to do so, there is no way we can make him make a statement until proceedings have started. You cannot start a case on the speculation that someone might be prepared to tell you what happened. If the witnesses are somehow involved, even on the periphery, then they are reluctant to assist. If they have skeletons in their cupboard, as many of them have, they are extremely reluctant to give evidence.

In 1985 the Bank of England came up with a good idea in suggesting the establishment of a commercial and financial crime division of the High Court, which would have its own procedures and would call on a specialist trial judiciary and expert lay assessors. The Bank told the Roskill Commission investigating procedures for dealing with serious fraud:

> A qualified experienced court may be able to dispose of cases more rapidly with beneficial effects on the resource and other costs incurred by those responsible for fraud prevention. The case for extending the coverage in this way would be supported by the argument that speedy and effective prosecution for regulatory offence is likely to nip in the bud that which might otherwise develop into fraud.

The Bank also added its weight to those who have criticized the government for failing to provide sufficient resources to the fight against corporate crime:

> The authorities must have adequate specialist resources at their disposal at the stage of investigation, and must be secure in their ability both to obtain evidence and, above all, to prevent its destruction or dispersal . . . reforms of judicial proceedings are unlikely in themselves to prove a sufficient deterrent to those contemplating the perpetration of serious frauds . . . the preser-

> vation of the City's reputation is dependent upon the efficicacy of investigations and procedures pre-trial as well as reforms of the pre-trial process itself.

The Roskill Committee accepted this advice, and in early 1986 recommended changes in the law, including the abolition of jury trial in complex city fraud cases.

10 Can It All Go Sour?

'What will the service industries be servicing when there is no hardware, when no wealth is actually being produced? We will be servicing, presumably, the production of wealth by others. We will supply the Changing of the Guard, we will supply the Beefeaters around the Tower of London. We will become a curiosity' – Lord Weinstock, chief executive of GEC.

'Because institutional shareholders predominate in the securities markets, many managements have little real sense of identification with the objectives of their shareholders. Nor do fund managers have the expertise to solve problems of underperformance by the companies in which they hold shares, so they resort to selling out. The takeover bid thus becomes a widely used device to cure corporate woes' – Sir Hector Laing, Chairman of United Biscuits.

Labour's Way

The Labour Party complains that since the abolition of exchange controls in 1979 huge amounts of capital have fled the country, and that this overseas investment has helped competitors abroad build more efficient factories, which, in turn, produce goods that push British products out of the market. This is perfectly true, for in the first five years after the abolition of controls more than £50bn. of portfolio investment found its way into overseas stocks. But it is not a purely British phenomenon; huge investment in Mexico, for example, diverted money away from the US automotive industry to such an extent that US car workers took huge pay cuts in order to keep their plants alive. There is no evidence that British car workers are prepared for a similar sacrifice.

Nor is it clear what would have happened had such investment been prohibited. There is no real evidence that it would have found its way into British industry. Had there not been a capital outflow, the pound would have been even stronger in the early 1980s, adding to industry's export competitiveness problems.

However, Labour's latest policy is to strip pension funds of their taxation privileges unless they agree to cut back foreign investment to about half its present level of around 15 per cent of total portfolios. Again, this may well prove totally ineffective in achieving Labour's aim of increasing the amount of money invested in British industry. It would be fairly easy for fund managers to increase their stakes in British companies with substantial foreign businesses, such as BP, ICI, Unilever, and Hanson Trust, though this would create investment distortions.

Labour would try and force the funds to invest in Britain through a National Investment Bank, which would supposedly operate independently of Whitehall and Government, even though it would be subsidized by the taxpayer, and charge lower interest rates for projects deemed to be 'in the National interest'. One can just imagine these projects being identified – another billion pounds for Austin Rover to help it maintain a dwindling market share by launching a new small car, countless billions to bring British Telecom, British Gas, and British Airways 'back into their rightful position of public ownership', and a few more billions for industrial parks in depressed areas like Merseyside, the North East and Northern Ireland.

A blue print for just such a bank but with rather less politicized goals, has been drawn up by the National Economic Development Council, an organization whose meandering thought processes over the years have contributed little to the aspirations implied by its name. Yet the idea does have the backing of some powerful voices in the City, including the Bank of England and Sir John Baring, chairman of Baring Brothers and part-time chairman of the NEDC committee on finance for industry. A starting equity base of about £100m. would, so it is believed, enable it to gear up to lending of up to £2.5bn., far too modest a sum to achieve any of Labour's major ambitions.

Baring's committee suggests that if such a bank were to

be established its financing of industrial projects, both large and small, should be separated from any role it might have to make specific investments at the Government's request. It would provide funds for companies, wishing to embark on innovative projects and those on a recovery path, and there is also the suggestion that it could finance infrastructure projects such as roads, rail electrification, and the development of East Coast ports.

One has to have more than usual confidence in politicians to imagine that such a National Investment Bank would have genuine independence, and the outlook under such an economic regime is starting to look depressingly familiar.

Let us view things from a different perspective, and ask ourselves whether a National Investment Bank is needed at all or, if it is, whether it could not operate commercially within the confines of the City? Let us also assume that the City revolution produces the effects that its proponents say it will – a permanent increase in the numbers of those owning shares, much greater turnovers on the London capital markets, including the Stock Exchange, and a bigger share for Britain in international equity trading. All are possible, and the nation will benefit from the boost to the economy from the substantial extra employment in London; there is talk of 80,000 extra jobs.

Finally, let us also assume that world economic growth does not falter, but forges ahead for a few more years. This cannot be a foregone conclusion, but nor is it a vain hope. The fall in oil prices resulting from the near-collapse of the OPEC cartel will provide a substantial boost to growth in the world's major locomotive countries: the United States, Japan and West Germany. In general a 10 per cent cut in oil prices creates 0.25 per cent growth across the industrialized world. The Organization for Economic Cooperation and Development, in its outlook for 1986 and beyond, published in December, 1985, believes the chances are good for the recovery being sustained 'for some time to come'.

Through the late eighties there will have been further successful public flotations of state enterprises. There will be widespread foreign shareholdings in all, as was the case with British Telecom and British Gas, but so what? This is the reverse of capital outflow; it represents a commitment from foreigners prepared to invest in Britain, and, of course, it releases capital for other investments. The stock markets will also be absorbing the financing of the Channel Tunnel, which will both create jobs and make better use of resources.

It is also perhaps not too much to hope that other urgently needed national projects will be funded through the City. As the Confederation of British Industry has repeatedly warned the Government, Britain's industrial and domestic infrastructure is in an advanced state of decay, with spending urgently needed on new motorways, rail electrification, sewerage repairs and ports. The principal trunk route for heavy lorries carrying goods from Britain's industrial heartland to the East Coast port of Felixstowe is little more than a country lane. There seems no good reason why new trunk roads should not be paid for by the user, as is the case in France and Italy, with the capital raised in the City, probably through the Eurobond market. The reshaping of British Rail, with the Government owning the track, and leasing route rights to private operators, financed through the City – as suggested by *The Economist* – is another possibility.

The obstacle towards implementing such plans, which, of course, would release much-needed taxpayers' money for improvements to hospitals and the education service, is, one suspects, not to be found in the City, but in Downing Street, where the Government has been remarkably slow to harness private capital to fund public works, despite the success of many other countries in doing so. It seems improbable that the Government will want to set up a new institution to harness funds in the way the Baring committee of NEDC has suggested, and the Prime Minister has also indicated a reluctance to provide government guarantees for private loan capital, a necessary precondition to any funding of the kind proposed.

But the fact that the government may have lost its radical cutting edge – if it ever had one – does not mean industry will be starved of funds. Even when the London Stock Market was a much more parochial place than it is today, there was never any shortage of capital for worthwhile business ventures. The Wilson Committee investigated this very issue with commendable thoroughness, and gave the Stock Exchange a clean bill of health, despite the lack of appeal it held for investors at the time. More recently, through the Unlisted Securities Market and the Stock Exchange itself, capital has been found for hundreds of high risk ventures. Meanwhile, lame ducks, as varied as *The Daily Telegraph* Ltd and Westland plc, the helicopter manufacturer, have been saved from receivership by injection of new equity from overseas. There is no reason to doubt that they will be turned into profitable enterprises: one has the examples of Chrysler UK, rescued by Peugeot; Times Newspapers Ltd, salvaged by News International; TV AM, retrieved by Kerry Packer; and Dunlop, reshaped by BTR, as living proof of what can be achieved by a mixture of new equity capital and a determined management. In each case, these companies are now growing beyond the wildest dreams of those who had written them off a few years ago. Two of the companies were said to be unmanageable, yet new managements have transformed performance from the same, if smaller, workforce. So long as there are managements prepared to tackle a challenge, there will be no shortage of funds from the stock markets.

The Stock Market of the Future

As to the future of the share markets themselves, I suspect the change will be less radical than seems probable now. It will be easier for individuals to buy shares, and maintaining a portfolio will be as simple as operating a bank account; indeed most banks will soon be offering their customers investment portfolio accounts, in much the same way as they market household budget accounts to spread the load of major bills evenly throughout the year. The banks will offer customers who agree to buy and sell shares or unit trusts through them regular statements evaluating a portfolio according to the latest prices, an investment advisory service, and individual financial counselling. These services may be free to those who agree to maintain certain balances, otherwise they will be on a fee-paying basis. Customers will be able to 'save' regularly by transferring a sum of money from their current account to their investment account, where the money will be put on 'high-interest' deposit until such time as shares are bought. The proceeds of shares sold will automatically be placed into the same interest-bearing account, unless the customer decides otherwise.

Building societies, to, will get in on the act. Under new legislation, they may lend a limited amount of money for purposes other than housing, and offer other financial services, such as investment advice. They may also become limited liability companies, and be taken over. With 26 million customers and 7,000 branches across Britain, they are likely to be snapped up by the new conglomerates as useful nationwide retail outlets for their services.

The High Street banks and building societies will thus become a dominant force in tapping the small investor market, and are likely to gain new business for the stock markets. So will department stores, where a limited number of outlets already exist for the sale and purchase of stocks and shares. Debenhams has opened money shops in a number of its stores, and these offer an estate agency, an insurance and a hire purchase facility, and investment advice. At the company's Oxford Street store, Quilter Goodison, the chairman of the Stock Exchange's own firm, has established a branch, where it offers what it likes to call 'free and disinterested' financial advice to all comers. The advice is presumably not so disinterested as to deter investors, who will then swiftly find out that it is far from free, for Quilter Goodison charge 1.65 per cent commission on any shares traded, with a minimum fee of £15. The Oxford Street experiment has been a considerable success, and each lunchtime a queue normally forms at the counter as customers line up to buy and sell equities.

What will happen to the average stockbroker, you may ask? The simple answer is that the average stockbroker has already disappeared. As explained earlier, most of the large City firms have been absorbed into financial conglomerates, which will wallow around in the fish tank together until the forces of competition bring further mergers, collapses, or the carving-out of numerous specialist niches. There is no way that all those authorized by the Bank of England to act as market-makers in the gilt-edged market can make a living from doing so. But the Bank decided that rather than make a choice itself from the suitable applicants, it would let the market make the judgement, and so be it.

The large conglomerates may expect to attract extra business, however, as a result of offering lower commission rates for orders telephoned, where the investor quotes a credit card number, rather as in ordering a package holiday, and where no advice is sought or given. Business will also come in through computer links with investment shops, where the conglomerate acts as a wholesaler, in an arrangement not dissimilar to that between a tour operator and a High Street travel agent. Competitive commission rates will also lead to increased turnover, particularly among professional and the wealthier personal investors.

The smaller stockbrokers are likely to witness the most change. Those who have enjoyed a good living on fixed commissions by picking up business from small networks and personal contacts may find life difficult. Many firms that fall within this category have already scrambled for cover under the umbrella of a larger firm. Others will thrive by offering particularly good service, by concentrating hard on the needs of individual customers, or by specializing. It seems to me a specialist brokers in certain areas: electronics, technology, Pacific Basin, communications, entertainment, and other areas where specialist knowledge is at a premium and where research work is important in valuing the potential of companies within the sector. In the case of subject specialities, these brokers will straddle the globe, for there are very few companies that can afford not to operate on an international scale.

If he is enterprising enough, the provincial broker will gain a new lease of life. Many regional brokers are able to act as market-makers in the shares of the companies they know well, and all have instant access to the SEAQ trading system. This means they are no longer the Stock Market's second-class citizens. I envisage another role for them also – the rebuilding of genuine mini stock markets, leading to a return to the philosophy of the great age of railways – raising finance for regional enterprise. They might, in fact, provide a smaller version of the successful Unlisted Securities Market, raising capital for business projects and for some worthy public projects. In the United States local bond issues are common for raising money for school assets, such as a swimming pool, or a sports centre. If the theory and practice of capital-raising on the London Stock Exchange for large projects mentioned earlier were replicated on a much smaller scale in country cities and towns, a whole new industry might emerge to challenge the dead hand of provincial banking.

Pensions for the Individual

Another large and expanding use for the Stock Market will be the Government's plans to encourage individuals to organize their own pension schemes. Employees will have the right to leave the State Earnings Related Pension Scheme (SERPS) or employer pension schemes, and gain significant tax benefits by organizing a personal scheme, which will be fully portable. Thus when an employee changes jobs, he will no longer suffer the disadvantage of losing his pension, especially the amount his employer has contributed. Both he and any employer will contribute to a lifelong individual scheme, which may be run by banks, building societies and unit trusts as well as life assurance companies and pensions' companies.

At one stage the Government had planned to phase out SERPS altogether, which would have resulted in extra funds being available to the Stock Market for investment amounting from 1990 onwards to between £500m, and £1.25bn. But it shrank from such a radical step, and at the time of writing it is unclear how much the market may be expected to gain.

New Competition

I do not doubt that the Stock Market will thrive, even under a change of Government. A future Labour Cabinet would probably end up being as pragmatic as the last one, when James Callaghan did his best to jettison any policy that smacked of Leftism. The fear of losing one of the few growing industries in Britain – and with it many thousands of City jobs as well as a flight of capital – would probably provide sufficient deterrent.

The Japanese Government has just embarked on a major

programme of deregulation, and Tokyo financial houses are training more young people than ever before. It is inevitable that the Tokyo Stock Exchange and other financial markets in Japan will gain in stature and size. Ten years ago Japanese fund managers and market operators had a reputation for excessive caution and no imagination.

Take Nomura Securities, for instance. From its unpretentious headquarters in Tokyo it spreads its tentacles across every continent, with offices in 28 cities in 19 countries. It is by far the world's richest and biggest securities house, earning more profits than Barclays Bank and J. P. Morgan combined.

In 1986 it chose London as the location of one of two world regional centres (the other was New York). Its declared aim is to become the dominant financial institution in every area of business everywhere – and it is clear that it, and its domestic rivals, Yamaichi, Nikko and Daiwa, pose as great a threat to the City as Sony and NEC have been to the electronics industry, and Toyota, Nissan and Honda to the motor industry.

I have no doubt that by 1990 the name of Nomura will become as well known in Britain as Natwest – it may by then have swallowed up one of the High Street banks. It has the will to succed, and is going about it the right way, slowly, painstakingly, and without fuss. In 1986 it was the largest single hirer of Oxbridge graduates on the annual 'milk run', ousting Unilever, Shell, ICI and BP from the top spot. These new recruits were flown to Tokyo for six months training, and quickly became enthusiastic about their new employer.

'I joined Nomura because I think their global expansion programme is absolutely phenomenal, and I am very sure they are going to come up number one way ahead of the others', said Christopher. 'They are going to be very big', said Catherine, 'they are very ambitious, and the togetherness and the spirit really is obvious'. 'They really believe in team work', said James, 'yet I am also amazed at the degree of responsibility that last year's graduates have been given. I can see myself making a very positive contribution to Nomura's profits'.

Didn't any of these young Britons feel uneasy that their country's own institutions might suffer as a result of the sheer force of Nomura's thrust? All scoffed at the suggestion, and James held up a white Nomura carrier bag.

'I joined a Japanese institution for precisely that reason', he said. 'I have brought this to show you because it sums up Nomura's attitude. It says "Nomura makes money makes money". Now a British institution would probably have a Latin ode or something, but Nomura knows what it is up to in the City.'

It certainly does. It has ruthlessly attacked the bond market, and is rivalling the American market leaders by offering cut prices. It has bought the vast old Post Office headquarters in St Martins Le Grand, and in early 1987 had preserved the facade but gutted the interior as part of a plan to build one of London's most impressive head offices. And its gradually building its local staff, supplementing their knowledge with the immense back up resources of the Nomura Research Institute, a think-tank just outside Tokyo with 500 staff – scientists and technologists as well as economists and analysts.

Nomura will be just one prong in the Japanese government's determination to gain a position in the world's financial services industry equivalent to the country's economic power.

Tokyo's market is already the second largest in the world, with over $700m. worth of shares traded in 1985, more than in the whole of Europe, including Britain. In April 1985, coming from behind Britain and operating with startling speed, given the conservative and consensus style of Japanese politics, Japan has already had its own version of the Big Bang. In 1985 broker commissions were slashed by 50 per cent, and soon they will be open to negotiation. Foreign investment houses have been allowed to operate in Tokyo, and a number of overseas banks have been given trust bank status, allowing them to compete for the nation's huge pensions business. And international stockbrokers have been allowed seats on the Tokyo Exchange – at a price, estimated at about £5m. a firm. To no one's surprise the first in was Merrill Lynch, thirsting to compete with Japan's own Big Four.

Tokyo's brokers already work long hours in a vigorous market, and Merrill's arrival in February 1986 provides sharp competition. 'As we begin executing and clearing our own trades in the Tokyo Exchange, we will have taken a major step towards opening a truly global market to each of our clients', proclaimed a full-page advertisement in the *Wall Street Journal*. With more international stocks being traded in Tokyo as well as New York, London will feel the competition, and it is very possible that the London Stock Market will be squeezed at both ends of the business day and lose both trading volume and value. Swift action by the Government to abolish stamp duty may help, but with 20 global firms, mostly American, dominating the international market it will be a remarkable feat if London can hold its own, and if it does so it will almost certainly be at the expense of the inefficient European bourses rather than by winning business away from the two giants.

Even the inefficiency of European exchanges may prove a problem, however. Common sense dictates that Amsterdam, Milan, Paris and Frankfurt are not going to let London have everything its own way. The Europeans will either compete, or seek a European Community solution through a common standard, which could provide London with the worst kind of nightmare – the bureaucratic kind. The Dutch capital markets are being liberalized, but the interesting changes are taking place in West Germany, where bank finance has long over-shadowed equities as the major source of capital for industry. The German banks have traditionally not only lent large sums of money to industrial giants, but have also taken stakes in companies and seats on the boards. Steps are now being taken to boost the role of the German bourses, particularly in attempting to assist the financing of small and medium-sized companies, and to encourage more small companies to make a public share issue.

Europe is small beer, however, and one has only to look at the figures to realize that the real competition for London will come from New York and Tokyo. A recent survey carried out for the European Commission found that in a comparison of fees on a $150,000 order Milan was 32 per cent dearer than the typical American fee, including taxes, while the cost in Britain was as much as 300 per cent higher. British costs will come down with the ending of fixed commissions, but not by sufficient to compete.

A Third Wave?

It is quite possible to be pessimistic about London's chances in a dogfight with New York and Tokyo, but, although American or Japanese brokers are not sentimental about London, conversations with numerous market players in both cities convince me that they want the British markets to play an important part in global securities trading, provided, of course, the political atmosphere, Conservative, Labour or Alliance, remains welcoming.

There is another, perhaps more distant, prospect that causes me to be optimistic about London, and that is the opportunities that are available to it to become the fulcrum of emerging equity markets in the Third World. These opportunities exist not because Britain is at the centre of the Commonwealth, but because of London's location in the world's central time zone. This may be a fanciful notion, for there are few pundits in 1986 who would be prepared to be optimistic about the prospects for the economies of Africa and the Middle East. Yet it is because all the collectivist approaches to finance in the Third World have failed so dismally that it is not too far-fetched to hope that soon the governments of developing nations will learn that an equity market may prove to be better at allocating resources than present methods. They will not learn this from bodies like the United Nations, but the success of fledgling markets in South East Asia, and the growth of the Japanese capital market since World War II, will surely serve as examples. Now that many high-growth Asian countries are taking lessons from City institutions about how to set about privatizing their state oligarchies, the days when a country's development was built round the inefficiencies of planning officers and the rigidities imposed by dull commercial banks, may be drawing to an end. Debt finance has brought with it seemingly unsurmountable problems.

The equity markets of the non-OECD world are not large, but many have grown big enough to offer solid long-term prospects. By mid-1985 they had a total market capitalization of $130bn., representing 10 per cent of all markets outside the United States. In Asia, Latin America and the Middle East, there are at least 35 of them, but most have not played a central role in financial systems because of over-reliance on debt finance and excessive regulations. Yet several of them are comparable in size with some European markets. The Hong Kong, Kuwait and Singapore markets are comparable in size with the American Stock Exchange, the second largest exchange in the United States, or the bourses in Paris and Geneva. They are far larger than most other Continental European markets, even the $20 – $25bn. markets of Amsterdam and Milan. The major Latin American markets of Brazil, Chile and Mexico, and the four largest markets in Asian developing countries – Malaysia, India, Taiwan and South Korea – are comparable to the markets of Spain, Belgium and Scandinavia. Turnover on these markets is also high; in some Asian countries an amount equivalent to 50 per cent of the stock changes hands each year.

It would be in the interest of the British Stock Exchange to assist in the development of some of these markets by offering advice, and providing facilities for secondments to London. So long as a country has political stability, a growing economy, well-developed auditing and accounting standards, and an adequate legal framework, there is no reason why a Stock Market should not flourish.

But if the City is to succeed it must work collectively as well as competitively. In the months immediately before and after 'Big Bang' the forces of rivalry seemed to me far greater than any spirit of enthusiasm for the common good; indeed such sentiment seemed strangely absent from the Square Mile, almost as if no one really cared what the rest of the British or global public thought.

Under a siege of criticism in the first half of 1987, the City appeared to adopt a siege mentality. Yet as the Deputy Chairman of the new Stock Exchange, Stanislas Yassukovich, put it to me:

> The City must spend more time talking to the rest of the world rather than to itself. We are too inward looking, and too inbred, if you like. We have got to bring Throgmorton Street to the High Street. If you travel around the United States, in almost every regional news programme, there are at least two or three daily stock market reports. Schools have investment clubs. Wall Street goes out and talks to them and to women's groups. Have

> you heard of a London stockbroker addressing a Women's Institute meeting? I am sure it has happened, but I must say I have never heard of it.

To me, that says it all.

Postscript

'We spend our days in issuing debt and retiring equity – both in record volumes – and then we spend our evenings raising each other's eyebrows with gossip about signs of stress in the financial system' – Paul Volcker, chairman Federal Reserve Board.

The shelves of the bookshops at Heathrow Airport are always well stocked with fiction predicting a global financial crash, whereas bookstores in Manhattan offer similar-sounding titles – but in the non-fiction section. There is no reason to suppose that the gloomy predictions of publications in either will come true. 1979 proved Paul Erdman wrong, while 1985 was a bad year for Wall Street's own Dr Doom, Henry Kaufman. Some of the ingredients are there for a repeat of the Wall Street crash, which if it happened, would also bring down Throgmorton Street, but although 1986 man is as motivated by greed as the 1929 variety, he is also better informed and protected.

The impact of 'Big Bang' will not be immediate. It will evolve from the next bear market, when, faced with a drooping market, competitive men will become desperate men. In such a market the US and Japanese conglomerates will prove to be the most efficient. It could be a repeat of Britain's much heralded entry into the European Community, which, the politicians promised, would breathe new life into our manufacturing industries. Instead, with a falling share of world markets, British industry became a shadow of its former self. I fear the City, too, is not that well-prepared for competition. It has had no choice but to act the way it has done, but it has hastened to change too slowly, as a result of which the global financial giants are poised to take over. A few of our stockbroking companies will survive as British, but the dominant force by the end of this decade will be American and Japanese. When I was at school there were nine British mainstream car manufacturers – Austin, Morris, MG, Riley, Rootes, Rover, Triumph, Jaguar and Wolseley – and two American – Ford and Vauxhall. The British-owned companies had 75 per cent of the market. Now there are only two British manufacturers, with less than 20 per cent market share. By 1990 it is possible, even likely, that, like the motor trade, three-quarters of the London securities market will be outside British hands. Does that matter, as long as Londoners have jobs? The answer, I fear, is that the big global markets will grow strongest where the capital is, and that, by 1990, the market capitalization in the United States and Japan will so predominate as to leave our Stock Market on the periphery.

Can this decline be arrested? Only, I would suggest, by the Government declaring the City a tax-free enterprise zone, ending stamp duty on transactions, abolishing capital transfer and capital gains taxation, and ending the present tax discrimination in favour of property investments and building societies. Even that will be insufficient to reverse the market forces stacked against London, unless the City itself becomes much more enterprising and imaginative in the creation and selling of new financial instruments, sheds for good its old-boy image, and sets about restoring its tarnished image as a place of insider traders and avaricious young people. In the end, if we want London to remain in the big league of capitalism, we have to behave like capitalists. And with capitalistic power comes capitalistic responsibility.

Index